The Best
Women's Stage Monologues
of 2006

Smith and Kraus *Books for Actors*
MONOLOGUE AUDITION SERIES
The Best Men's / Women's Stage Monologues of 2005
The Best Men's / Women's Stage Monologues of 2004
The Best Men's / Women's Stage Monologues of 2003
The Best Men's / Women's Stage Monologues of 2002
The Best Men's / Women's Stage Monologues of 2001
The Best Men's / Women's Stage Monologues of 2000
The Best Men's / Women's Stage Monologues of 1999
The Best Men's / Women's Stage Monologues of 1998
The Best Men's / Women's Stage Monologues of 1997
The Best Men's / Women's Stage Monologues of 1996
The Best Men's / Women's Stage Monologues of 1995
The Best Men's / Women's Stage Monologues of 1994
The Best Men's / Women's Stage Monologues of 1993
The Best Men's / Women's Stage Monologues of 1992
The Best Men's / Women's Stage Monologues of 1991
The Best Men's / Women's Stage Monologues of 1990
One Hundred Men's / Women's Stage Monologues from the 1980s
2 Minutes and Under: Character Monologues for Actors Volumes I, II, and III
Monologues from Contemporary Literature: Volume I
Monologues from Classic Plays 468 BC to 1960 AD
100 Great Monologues from the Renaissance Theatre
100 Great Monologues from the Neo-Classical Theatre
100 Great Monologues from the 19th Century Romantic and Realistic Theatres
The Ultimate Audition Series Volume I: 222 Monologues, 2 Minutes & Under
The Ultimate Audition Series Volume II: 222 Monologues, 2 Minutes & Under
from Literature

YOUNG ACTOR MONOLOGUE SERIES
Cool Characters for Kids: 71 One-Minute Monologues
Great Scenes and Monologues for Children, Volumes I and II
Great Monologues for Young Actors, Volumes I and II
Short Scenes and Monologues for Middle School Actors
Multicultural Monologues for Young Actors
The Ultimate Audition Series for Middle School Actors Vol.I: 111 One-Minute
Monologues
The Ultimate Audition Series for Teens Vol. I: 111 One-Minute Monologues
The Ultimate Audition Series for Teens Vol. II: 111 One-Minute Monologues
The Ultimate Audition Series for Teens Vol. III: 111 One-Minute Monologues
The Ultimate Audition Series for Teens Vol. IV: 111 One-Minute Monologues
The Ultimate Audition Series for Teens Vol. V: 111 One-Minute Monologues
from Shakespeare
Wild and Wacky Characters for Kids: 60 One-Minute Monologues

If you require prepublication information about upcoming Smith and Kraus books, you may receive our semiannual catalogue, free of charge, by sending your name and address to *Smith and Kraus Catalogue, PO Box 127, Lyme, NH 03768. Call us toll-free (888) 282-2881 or visit us at www.smithandkraus.com.*

The Best
Women's Stage Monologues
of 2006

edited by D. L. Lepidus

MONOLOGUE AUDITION SERIES

A SMITH AND KRAUS BOOK

Published by Smith and Kraus, Inc.
177 Lyme Road, Hanover, NH 03755
www.SmithandKraus.com

First Edition: November 2006
10 9 8 7 6 5 4 3 2 1

Cover illustration: *Wardrobe* by Lisa Goldfinger
Design and production by Julia Hill Gignoux

The Monologue Audition Series
ISSN 1067-134X
ISBN 1-57525-555-3

NOTE: These monologues are intended to be used for audition and class
study; permission is not required to use the material for those purposes. However, if there is a paid performance of any of the monologues included in
this book, please refer to the Rights and Permissions pages 107–113 to lo-
cate the source that can grant permission for public performance.

CONTENTS

FOREWORD

In these pages, you will find sixty terrific monologues, all from recently published plays. Included on the Rights and Permissions pages is information as to who published each play, so if you like a piece in this book, the entire text will be easy to track down. Although there are some wonderful monologues for women "of a certain age," most of the pieces in this book are appropriate for acting students in their twenties or early thirties. There are, however, some fine monologues here for high and middle schoolers. Something for everyone from Smith and Kraus!

Here, you will find monologues from plays by the finest contemporary playwrights, such as Theresa Rebeck, Ken Ludwig, Don Nigro and Paul Weitz, who have achieved considerable success in the theater, and work from exciting newcomers such as Danai Gurira, Nikkole Salter, Jonathan Rand, Doug Rand, Robert Pridham, and Joseph Goodrich, in a variety of styles.

I was chastised last year, in a generally favorable review of the 2005 monologue books, for not including enough comic pieces — so with considerable effort I have found several for this year's books. Why "with considerable effort"? you might well ask. Well, because published plays tend to come from America's nonprofit theaters, where (it seems) everything has to be dark and disturbing and oh-so-terribly "cutting-edge." I hope you will find enough comic monologues in this book to suit your needs; but if you need to keep looking I highly recommend one of Smith and Kraus' recent publications, *The Ultimate Monologue Book, Volume IV: 222 Comedy Monologues 2 Minutes & Under*, edited by John Capecci and Irene Ziegler Aston, a wonderful selection of contemporary and classical pieces.

I have had the honor of editing Smith and Kraus' annual *Best Monologues* series since 2001. I think this year's edition is the best yet; but ultimately, that's for you to say.

— *D. L. Lepidus*

ACT A LADY
Jordan Harrison

Comic
Romola's Ghost, any age

> *Act a Lady is a comedy about a group of men in a small town who decide to put on a play, acting all the roles — male and female. In the original production, this role was played by a man. The character is the ghost of a character in the play-within-the-play.*

> *(Romola's Ghost enters, hot on her trail, but seemingly in no hurry. Her movements are dreamy but demented. She seems almost to float. She is very very pale.)*

ROMOLA'S GHOST: Buried me face down in the earth, buried me emeraldless and husbandless looking down toward China but I still clawed my way out. Scratch scratch scratch, nails to coffin satin — griming and dirting and earthing underneath my filed fine fingernails 'till I wormed my way out. Followed a worm up and broke through to the sun. Only it wasn't sunning out, it was mooning, full-mooning in the Pére Lachaise.

> *(She runs Valentino's crimson ascot through her hands.)*

Got a pretty pretty blood red pretty for my collection, now I'm searching a snood if you find a snood you find the girl to go with it. The girl. The girl. The girl won't have no using for a snood no more when I'm through with eating the space between her chin and her collarbone, her snoodplace, boring through that soft soft girl 'till you hit spine.

Dead don't talk quite the same sort as the living no more but the words are still enough, you understand? Imperfect speeching not so ladylike with the commas sounding in the wrong place but it's what feels good in my mouth these days and I wonder if it'll speak denser the longer I'm decay.

> *(Looking at the ascot, again.)*

Believed you, Valentino. Trusted you madly but instead he played

1

goosey-loosey with my jewel and my heart and now I want my right-ful emerald back, I want, I want. Wasn't hardly knowing what I wanted from life-ing, but the after is ever clearer as crystal-clear. And it's good to have a purposeful, even if the flesh is creeping toward purple. But if six feet of dirt couldn't stop me then no chamber whore nor any of yous won't don't stop me no

mark
my —
Worrrrd.

ACT A LADY
Jordan Harrison

Comic
Lorna, thirties to forties

> Act a Lady *is a comedy about a group of men in a small town who decide to put on a play, acting all the roles — male and female. They have enlisted some of the ladies in their community to help, including Lorna, who is doing their makeup.*

LORNA: The first start to being pretty is powder for that nice even tone. Don't know nobody who gotta nice even tone without the helpa powder 'cept maybe the China-woman who works down in the laundry. Asked her once how she gets such fine even tone and she touched my cheek — her hand just shot out from behind the counter and stretched my cheek-skin between her thumb and pointer finger like that, and she said: "Peaches and cream." Peaches and cream is all she said but I knew somehow that meant "You're all right, Lorna — you be happy with what you got." That was nice. But that's a whole other story.

First start to being pretty is powder and you use the powder puff here, puff puff puff anywhere and everywhere but 'specially wherever it's — darn it, darn it. Darn it I shoulda started you all with shaving. Shaving for the boys, gotta shave real close first or else you'll end up looking like you're some kinda sideshow act let out on the loose — which is OK if that's what you want but that's not what we want. Illusion we want. Elegant we want. Ladies we want.

I know, I'm a dreamer, I know, that's what they call me. But I think when we get all your wives and sisters and mom-folk lined up opening night they're going to see I've been dreaming real. Now, third step after shave 'n powder is gonna be your eyes. Big big eyes to put Pickford to shame. You do wanna look pretty, right fellas?

ALL IN LITTLE PIECES
John Yearley

Dramatic
Mary, could be any adult age, but probably thirties to forties

Mary reveals her dark secrets to Molly, a total stranger who is thinking of buying her house.

MARY: You know, come to think of it, I think my marriage was a marriage of convenience, too. . . .

　　I used to think so. Now I'm not so sure. I think I was very convenient to have around. Like at his parties. He used to have these big, lavish parties. God, I can see him sitting at the head of the table right now. Telling all his little stories and jokes. Sometimes they were about me, you know. He would tell some story about how stupid I was and everyone would just laugh their heads off. Like he used to tell this one about how I didn't know that JFK and John Kennedy were the same person. Like that's the funniest thing in the world. And all his friends would just bust a gut laughing at me. I would laugh, too. I would. I didn't know what else to do. Funny thing is, that was actually the best part of the evening. Because when I went to bed, no matter how late it was, he would throw me down on the bed, facing forward, with my hair grabbed in a clump in his fist. And he would whisper this dirty talk in my ear. If I didn't say anything back he'd grab my hair tighter and say, "You like that?! Huh?" So I'd say "yeah" or "fuck me" or whatever he wanted. Anything to make it stop. As soon as he had finished he would collapse, maybe give me a good shove so I would stay off his half of the bed. And when he got up, at noon, it would be like nothing had ever happened. House clean. Lunch prepared. Wife smiling. Very convenient. For him, anyway. *(Pause. Mary opens her purse and pulls out a flask.)* Do you want a drink? I could sure use one. *(Mary takes a long drink.)* I'm sorry. I've probably offended you again, haven't I? Some pathetic housewife spewing out her problems. . . .

    (Pause.) You know, sometimes I don't think I'll miss this house one little bit. Sometimes I just want to beat and claw at it until there's nothing left.

ARE WE THERE YET?
Garth Wingfield

Comic
Amanda, early thirties

> *In this direct address to the audience, Amanda talks to the audience about her unhappiness with her life.*

AMANDA: *(To audience.)* Amanda's career. A farce in one act.
(She opens a copy of The Little Engine That Could *and reads to us.)*
AMANDA: *(Continues, as if to a roomful of children.)* "And the Little Blue Engine thought of the good little boys and girls on the other side of the mountain who would not have any toys or good food unless she helped. Then she said, 'I think I can. I think I can. I think I can.' " *(Looks up, at her audience.)*
    Isn't this a nice story?

    Yes, Marietta? No, I don't know where your agent is. She's probably checking your lighting or something.

    Hugo? No, I can't run lines with you right now. I'm doing this.

    Actually, um, cast . . . I wanted to tell you that today is my last day with you for a while. It's been wonderful working with you, but I'm going off to the hospital to have an operation, and I'm not sure when I'll be back.

    No, Carmen, it's not cosmetic.

    Anyway, in my absence, Joseph will be your network talent executive. You all remember Joseph, right?

    That's right, Shirley, the gay guy.

No, Howard, I'm afraid he already has a boyfriend. And you're *nine*, Howard, so that's really very . . .

Do I have a boyfriend? OK, let's see, that would be a big fat no. I had one, but he, well . . . he had issues, so we broke up. Anyway, getting back to the *Little Blue Engine* . . .

What, Genevieve? Well, yes, I suppose I would like to get married someday, only I have to find the right person and fall in love first, now don't I?
(More irritated now.)
No, Marcus. I have plenty of time.

Tell you what, let's just listen to the story and save our questions for later, OK?
(Reading again.)
"Puff, puff, chug, chug, went the Little Blue Engine. 'I think I can, I think I can, I think I can . . .' "

THE AUDITIONERS
Doug Rand

Comic
Auditioner #3, probably twenties

> *This play is a comedy about the audition process for actors. Speaker is an actress doing a contemporary monologue.*

AUDITIONER #3: My contemporary monologue is from *Grabbing the Sash* by Kristen Neander.
> *(And #3 begins.)*

I just want to thank you all so much for giving me the opportunity to become your Queen. If selected, I promise a reign of peace, prosperity, and boundless happiness, and also I'll do my best to represent our town at nationals. But first, I'd like to let you know a little bit more about me.

My favorite color is magenta.

My favorite season is summer.

My favorite country is America.

My favorite animal is puppies.

My height is [X]'[X]". *(Use whatever numbers are plausible for this actor.)*

My weight is [XX] pounds, of which I am understandably proud.

My measurements are [XX-XX-XX], which are also a source of great satisfaction to myself and others.

My Web site is iamindeedhot.com, where you can gain a deeper appreciation of the previous information.

My screen name is Slinkyminx287, and I like to chat about grown-up things.

My birthday is [XX-XX-XXXX], so as of three weeks ago, this kind of chatting is totally legal.

My phone number is unlisted, but you'll find it on the back of my headshot.

And now, for the brainiac portion of this pageant, I chose the following question: "Why must human beings always suffer?" I thought about this question really hard, since my answer counts for fifty points, which is more than the swimsuit portion — and the more I thought about it, the more I realized it's a trick question.

Because really, the question should be, "Must human beings always suffer in the first place?" And I totally think the answer is "no." We're so smart, you know? (I'm talking about human beings in general, not specific individuals, like my idiot sister. [JK, Kaitlyn!]) If we can put a man on the moon and we can figure out that deadly toxic botulism is good for getting rid of wrinkles, then surely we have the tools to cure any disease, heal any infirmity, and enhance any mood.

THE AUDITIONERS
Doug Rand

Comic
Auditioner #2, teens to twenties

> *This play is a comedy about the audition process for actors. Speaker is an actress doing a contemporary monologue.*

AUDITIONER #2: My classical monologue is from the tragically underproduced masterwork of Natalie Stannard, entitled *Rosaline's Lament.*
> *(#2 begins:)*
>
> O Romeo, Romeo — I'm gonna hurt you, Romeo.
>
> I was looking forward to Uncle Capulet's party for *months!* And you said you were going to sneak in so that you could dance with *me.* If you can remember back that far. Back when you told me that I was the most beautiful girl in the world, and that your eyes were only for me, that you'd die without my smile.
>
> It feels like only yesterday you said these things. Oh, wait, that's because it *was* only yesterday, right before you suddenly decided that my loser cousin Juliet should get every last scrap of your attention.
>
> Frankly, Romeo, I'm disappointed. I question your judgment, really. Because guess what: Juliet's not that pretty. Her eyes are too far apart, and she wears too much makeup, and I know from way too many summers at sleepaway camp that she snores like a bear. Also, FYI, Romeo, she's thirteen. You may not see that as a problem, but we have certain laws in Verona you might want to think about before busting a move on little miss jailbait.
>
> Not that you care. You're probably laying the moves on Juliet right now, tonight of all nights: the tortured sighing. The balcony by moonlight. The rhymed couplets. Ungh, you are *so predictable.*
>
> And here you told me "the all-seeing sun ne'er saw my match since first the world begun." You wouldn't shut up about my bright eyes, my high forehead and my scarlet lip; my fine foot, straight leg

and quivering thigh; and the demesnes that there adjacent lie — not that you're getting anywhere near these demesnes without a ring, lover boy. Maybe Juliet is less persnickety on that front. Is that it, Romeo? Is that why you dropped me for a *thirteen-year-old who snores?!*

O Romeo, Romeo — you see me coming and you'd better run, Romeo.

What's in a name? that which we call an ass
By any other name would smell as foul.

You are so dead.

BODY TALK
Tanya Palmer

Dramatic
Character could be any age.

> Body Talk *is a monologue play dealing with women's issues of self-image.*

ONE: I see myself in a drugstore window. Tall. Wearing big boots that make me feel like I'm strutting everywhere I go. Supercool. Tight pants. Black. And I can't believe it's me 'cause I'm beautiful. I don't even recognize myself, and it's like a whole other individual has taken over my reflection. She's thin and she's got a big smile and she stands with her shoulders back, not crouching forward, and she looks mean through her happiness. Tough. And I love her. Love her. ME. I recognize that stupid shy scared sadness not quite ready to leave her face. And I hear her fear. What do you do when you've never liked yourself, never known how to. Always thought you were nothing good, only something to hide. But one day like magic you see yourself full of love for yourself like a spell has been cast. I see, touch, taste that face. My face. And my body and my beauty shines like a beam of light so bright I'm propelled forward, down the street and into a coffee shop. I enter with my big thick boots and flash a big smile at the girl behind the counter with the cat eyes and the golden hair. She's wearing a shirt that's sea foam, that's the color — sea foam. "I love your shirt." She smiles and says "thanks" and I'm feeling so sexy, like heat just at the surface of every part of me, she can feel it too. We exchange glances like it's too bad we're in a crowded coffee shop otherwise we could rip our clothes off, except my boots, and see just how fucking amazing we are. Everyone looks up and takes me in. I smile a huge, generous, I'm-giving-you-a-piece-of-me smile to this man with graying hair sitting on a black and pink stool and he smiles back. We are radiant, the two of us together, and me and the cat-eyed girl are radiant too. I turn again and flash my smile to the whole fucking place and they smile back and I think this, Thomas Merton, is an example of universal love. This is me saying I love myself so much I can love every single one of you, that's how much love I got in me. I buy a mochaccino 'cause it's the most expensive drink, and I love this and myself and I don't need anyone else to tell me why.

BODY TALK
Tanya Palmer

Dramatic
Character could be any age.

> Body Talk *is a monologue play dealing with women's issues of self-image.*

THREE: I'm trying. To be positive. If I don't I start having panic attacks. Don't look alarmed. Well, I guess it is alarming. It's alarming for me too. When suddenly I start to breathe really quick and shallow. Hyperventilating. I don't always know what starts it off, it's usually nothing concrete, it's something in my head, a thought like for example "That was the stupidest fucking thing you could have said." "Idiot FAT UGLY idiot." And from that point on I lose a sense of connection to real events. "You're stupid, you can't do anything, you'll never do anything, ever. Ever. Ever." And why not? It doesn't make any sense. I'm smart. I'm . . . I'm what? I'm not a fucking thing. I'm a vacuous vacuum. I'm a collection of sour gases. I'm a series of mistakes. That's when I start to hyperventilate. So I'll be positive, so I don't have to put you through that. So as not to alarm you. When I was growing up I went to the Unitarian church and they taught us this chant: I am lovable and capable. So as to empower the soul. If you love yourself, then you can love others. So the theory goes. So I say that to myself. I am lovable and capable. Or I change the order. I am capable and lovable. Or I say one without the other. I am capable. But am I lovable? And I look down at my body and it's been destroyed by my mind. The sour gases turn my skin sour. It's not smooth it's scaly, it's not tight, it bursts into hideous bubbles of white fat. FAT. I want to punish this fucking body for being so fucking ugly it makes me sick so I try different things, like sometimes I hit my head against the wall over and over again until I almost pass out. Or I punch myself in the gut or I just stare at my face and scrub at it hoping I can make it disappear. My body is covered in a cloak that says to people, stay away, 'cause if you get too close I'll contaminate you with my sour gases. But then I'm lonely so I say to that face in words that slice through flesh, "You're incapable incapable incapable of making friends. No one could ever love you. You're unlovable because you're nothing but badness." So if you want to know why I'm hyperventilating it's 'cause if I didn't force myself to breathe I'd stop. My body is making one last effort to bring my mind back to life. All I can do is cry or scream 'cause that's how much I hate me. The sour juices are stewing and simmering inside. They whisper to my flesh. You have committed a terrible sin. How do I atone?

BOY ON BLACK TOP ROAD
Dale Wasserman

Dramatic
Donna, eighteen

Donna is talking to a boy, who may be an imaginary remembrance of her brother.

DONNA: All my life I've been a coward. There's reason, I guess . . . plenty reason to be scared. What's bad is that it makes you cruel. You turn cruel when somebody probes that little nest of fear you hide inside. You lash out with your claws, and you wound and you hurt whoever sees inside you. You can't bear that anyone should see that you're not cocky, you're afraid. But you are — of so many things. Of being hated . . . or loved. Of failure . . . and maybe of success. Of growing old. We're afraid of the dark before the lights come on. Then we're afraid of the light, what it might show. Afraid to die. Maybe more afraid of living. But of all the stuff there is to fear, I guess the worst is loneliness. *(A pause.)* . . .

Sure as hell, company doesn't help. If you want to find real Grade-A blue ribbon loneliness, try a crowd. Even a crowd of one. I have . . . oh, God, so many times. I'd be alone for a while, until the ache was right up in my throat and I'd be hollering without a sound, saying, "Know me. Discover me. I'm here, inside — somebody, *please.*" But they couldn't hear my silent voice, so after a while I'd be saying, "Make love to me." They didn't ask much. They didn't get much. *(She giggles.)* You wouldn't know about that. The big bad sex-express. "Love me, love me — well, if you can't love me, OK, fuck me." It's like a dance . . . all the moves have been rehearsed, you just follow the music. *(Singing, raucously.)* "Circle round and dosey do, All change partners, off we go!" *(Quietly again.)* And that's how it goes. Time after time after time. Reach out for love and find you've been stuck with sex. Booby-trapped by your own hormones!

THE DEAR BOY
Dan O'Brien

Dramatic
Elise, twenties

Elise, a teacher, is talking to an older, male teacher at a party.

ELISE: You teach: and you love it. And when you don't love it you at least feel proud. You've got a martyr's pride . . .

Because I'll tell you something: I'm good at it. Teaching. The kids *love* me — and I can't *stand* them. — I hate them — the *kids* — I hate "kids" . . . And the children at that school can all eat shit for all I care: I mean, this *attitude* they have — ? They look down on you as a matter of course, as if it's somehow *polite* of them to condescend to talk to you, because *you don't live there* — you can't *afford* to! — So I constantly feel this need to shock them, you know? To break them of their smug little complacencies — about life. I flirt with the boys; I wear low-cut blouses, leather minis. I'm a bitch to the girls; I confront them with symbolic gang-rape in *Lord of the Flies* — and they are *shocked!* — Thank God *something* shocks them!, for a moment, for a few days, they're confused, and violated . . . Why would she do this to us? What's Miss Sanger trying to *say* . . . ?

But they get used to it, don't they . . .

They've started to laugh at me already: "O, that's Miss Sanger" — they don't use the word *Ms.,* it's like their mouths are congenitally incapable of forming the sounds required — "That's our *Miss* Sanger for you: it's because she's *so young* . . ."

Don't get me wrong: it's me: I'm an artist — a novelist; by nature. That's what I wanted to be in the first place, when I got out — of college. I went to Brown? I wrote a novel as my senior thesis. It's not that good: too long — it's trite — Richard read it; he had *lots* of notes . . . It's not organic just yet, let's just put it that way; but it's a start . . . It's about a place, in case you're wondering, very much like

Brown: there's a murder, yadda yadda yadda . . . I haven't given up on it just yet . . . But once you grow up, and by "up" I mean twenty-six, -seven, you find you've got to pay your rent, right? You've got to get health insurance. You have *got* to get a life, so — wake up! You know? Get married, have kids quick before your ovaries dry up like a, like what? . . . fruit is so — *fuck!* . . . Anyway: and then you've got to find time to be inspired and isn't that just about the most depressing thing you've ever heard . . . ?

DEAR KENNETH BLAKE
Jacquelyn Reingold

Dramatic
Tina, thirties, an immigrant from Cambodia

Tina is in love with a homeless man, whom she has never met until now. She has been corresponding with him.

TINA: Maybe if we think things aren't going to work sometimes we do it anyway. Maybe we are just afraid. Maybe we think it cannot be different. You say Cambodia is far from here, but they write about it in *The New York Times.* And do you know what they write about now? They had elections this year. And this country is trying to help make peace there. How do they think they can do that — now? How can they think they can do that? I lose my family, my home, my country. I come here and see a man on TV, and he has the eyes of my father when they took him away. I watch him, and I feel a love for this man, this man I don't know, this man I am afraid will think I'm crazy if I tell him. I write him many letters, he writes me one back, I take a bus and I find him, and I see he does have those eyes, and I see — I can see — he has a soul like my family, and he doesn't smile when he looks at me, and he does not want the gifts I bring him, and he says he has no home, and I am afraid, and I do it any way. I ask him to take off his shoes, and when he says "no" I am again afraid, and I think it will not work, but I know, I know what I see, even if he doesn't, even if he will never know, I know, and I say, Dear Kenneth Blake, I say it anyway, if your feet hurt you take off your shoes and put them in the dirt. I ask for nothing else. Just that.

FIDDLE AND FADDLE
Tom Gliatto

Comic
Faddle, could be any age

> *This play is a wild political satire. Faddle is speaking to her companion, Fiddle.*

FADDLE: I am not superfluous. We are not superfluous. They also serve who — serve. We are, in our way, essential, or he would not have us here round the clock on red alert, so to speak, next to naked. Yes. And just remember this if you ever doubt your importance: You are giving the best years of your life to your country and to your president. Even if you do nothing but wait by the pool until he comes ambling in and throws us into the water and rips off our tops and has sex with us. *(Looking at her magazine again, but not relaxing.)* I am not ashamed to say I regard myself as a patriot. *(Puts the magazine down.)* And I will tell you — the greatest betrayal either of us could commit? If, by some preposterous and cruel turn of events, Castro were to take over the country, and he drove into Washington in his jeep and dusty beard and he were to say, "Fiddle and Faddle? This is Fidel! I am coming down to the pool to taste the succulent fruits that so delighted the president" — well, I would drown myself before he even removed his filthy underwear. And I would take you with me with my arms draped around your neck like heavy seaweed. No I will never ever sleep with a communist. Not even doze. Sleep with the president, and the president only, and be a patriot. Sleep with a communist and be a whore. "Punta" I think is the word. I mean, you can imagine the sort of girls he, Castro, keeps on hand to — Well, yes, as I said, puntas. Vicious girls from the country sleeping their way up the party ranks. Filthy little opportunists, which is a far cry from patriot. And, revolution being what it is, you can bet those girls will end up on the dustbin of history. Broken like the little pathetic dolls they are! There is no fidelity in Fidel. Ha! Whereas you and I, F and F, have been treated to night education classes at Vassar by the Secret Service, and finishing classes with the same woman who trained the first lady, and the president's doctor treats us routinely for the infections that are a regrettable consequence of the job. I think we could "pass," so to speak, in Hyannisport. Except that we're not allowed there, no of course not. Our place is here by the pool, expecting and then pleasuring the president. Imagine how the family would feel, after all, they're out playing touch football or sailing or some typical Irish Catholic activity, and who should stroll by but Fiddle and Faddle in their bikinis? Duty! Duty! Duty!

FIDDLE AND FADDLE
Tom Gliatto

Dramatic
Fiddle, could be any age

> *This play is a wild political satire. Fiddle is speaking to her companion, Faddle.*

FIDDLE: It's just — the thing that I find strange is . . . I have been sitting here thinking about nuclear weapons, and nuclear war, and all the children in the world being destroyed, reduced to cinders and curling up into a flaming sky. That was what I dreamed, that. All the cinders floating up, the way the air will stir them and suck them up in the fireplace and up out the chimney and into the night. Only they were babies. Little orange glowing fetuses. And I think of this one never getting a chance to see anything of life. There will be no world for it. And as a result I feel — a sadness that I have never. . . . — Think, Faddle, no world. No — circuses or Christmas wrapping or apple turnovers — I mean, those are simply happy associations of mine, they mean nothing in the larger scheme. Except that I associate them, too, with my mother, who was so good to me, to everyone. *(She is getting tearful, then.)* And I suspect would have had a significantly different take on patriotic duty than yours. Yet I will get rid of it, I will, the baby. In which case it will know nothing of anything, regardless. *(Sighs.)* I don't know. This *does* seem such a sad — conundrum? Or maybe not. I mean, you know — perhaps when the crisis is ended, and I am finished with the White House — I assume the president will tire of me while I am still somewhere in my reproductive years — maybe there will be *other* children I can have, only by some nonpolitical figure, an engineer or a businessman or minister and — oh, it just makes me *sad,* what can I say? *(Crying a little.)* Inexpressibly sad. And is it, is this sadness, is it new to me because nuclear war is new? Or because pregnancy is new? I can't parse out my feelings. . . .

Women, even mistresses, are *meant* to give life. Simple biology! Communist women too! Aren't there seven or six little Kruschevs? *I* was meant to give life. And here I am by a pool waiting for the president or waiting for death, and my poor mother died thinking I would probably settle down with Jeff, except for the Viet Cong, and that's assuming he actually didn't defect — and the Secret Service has given me this stupid name — and — and — I *am* superfluous, Faddle. I have been rendered superfluous. And I am not supposed to be! You know what? It's *women* who bring life into the world, and men who bring death. I am vital to the world, not the president. And also! Also — how can death be just a moment, as Marcus Aurelius says, or you say, or whoever, if everything is totally dead in the universe for all time? That is not a moment. That is eternity. I know the difference between eternity and a moment!

FUGITIVE PIECES
Caridad Svich

Dramatic
Downcast Mary, late teens to early twenties

> *Downcast Mary, a young homeless woman, confides in a young*
> *homeless man she's met named Troubled John about the first time*
> *she was caught stealing. This is a play told about the backyards of*
> *America haunted by dust bowl–era artifacts and an endless flow of*
> *immigrants undocumented and unrecorded by time.*

DOWNCAST MARY: . . . You know how much I stole? First time?
   A can of beans.
   I thought like you: "Stealing's wrong. God's law."
   But I'd been fire-walking for a good ten days . .
   Walking without stop, burning my soles, running.
   I was dead hungry.
   I thought "If I get picked up, at least it'd be some kind of sanctuary."
   So, I walk into this dime market that was lit like Christmas
   so there was no way a blue-coat could miss it.
   And I take a can of French-cut green beans, and slide it into my bag
   and I think "All right, all right," but there's nobody.
   I walk out of that store and there's not a sound.
   So, I turn into this little side yard,
   an ash-brown patch of grass,
   and start to bust open the can,
   when a runt comes down and breaks my back,
   pushes my face between his legs until I can't breathe,
   and I hear the sounds of the can hitting the ground,
   French-cut green beans snaking across the grass,
   and I'm bleeding.
   Next I know I'm in a blind place,
   my back feels like sharp metal's been put into it,
   and I haven't stopped being hungry.

Runt puts me on quinine for a week.

"This bird is quarantined," he said.

"She's suffering from malaria.

Pay no heed to what she says. She's got a head full of dreams.

Dreams and inventions. Cruel sort of disease."

Quinine stuck to my throat.

Every time I asked for water, all I got was a lime the size of a bull penny: flat and round.

And King Runt would come into me every night,

four and five times. See, he was a Bible man. He didn't like thieves.

When I got let out, I couldn't walk without falling to my knees.

Runt wrote down on some paper I had a "chemical deficiency,"

and there wasn't a doctor that could cure me.

He made me sign the paper with my teeth.

"Bit by an unlettered bird," he wrote,

"an unlettered daughter of the Kansas plains."

And then a spurred boot hit my rear

and landed me onto a blank street,

where every grain of light and dark

seemed to be reaching toward my eye.

I started to walk, but I was bleeding inside.

The blank street turned into a rough footpath.

The twilight's murmur hit my brow.

I could hear voices call out:

"How many dead? How many dead?"

A light fell on me. Skin-and-bone.

I looked up. And there were a hundred stars

hung in the sky like loose flowers on snow.

And I swore from that day on that they'd be my sanctuary.

And yes, I'd be a thief,

but I wouldn't take a can of beans,

I'd just take, and take, and take.

I'd out-thieve all the runts.

I'd dare them to catch me.

Cause I had the protection of the stars.

Only a constellation could cage me.

HALF-LIFE
Katy Darby

Dramatic
Jay, twenties to thirties

> *Jay, an English journalist, has kidnapped and is holding hostage*
> *Dirk, a former movie star who's now a U.S. Senator, to whom she*
> *is speaking.*

JAY: There's another meaning to half-life, by the way, which is relevant here.
If you've never heard of Oppenheimer I assume you don't know it,
so I'll tell you. The half-life of a radioactive substance is the length
of time — usually measured in years — that it takes for the ra-
dioactivity it emits to drop by half. Are you with me? . . .

So if you walked through Hiroshima the day after they dropped
Oppenheimer's baby, you would die of radiation sickness, whereas if
you returned fifty years later all you'd get is a higher risk of cancer.
Fame has a half-life, like anything else. Other stars shine brighter, and
pretty soon nobody can remember who Edmund Kean or Dan Leno
or Rosalind Franko were. The more famous, the longer the half-life.
Like if Shakespeare were a radioactive isotope, he'd probably be
strontium-90, which has a half-life of several hundred years. Bear with
me. . . .

I don't want to die but I haven't got a choice. Everybody dies,
some sooner than others. Tough shit. But I want people to remember my name. I want fresh flowers on that grave, or graffiti, barbed
wire, poison ivy, I don't care. Because being good doesn't get you remembered. It might get you to heaven if you can be bothered to believe in it but it doesn't get you in the history books. Most people
sublimate their desire to live forever by having children. They pass
on their genes and their work here is done. I'm told it makes you less
selfish. Got any kids? . . .

I don't either, as you have probably guessed, so no immortal DNA for me. But I want my fifteen minutes and more, and I'm running out of road. Any guesses at what I'm going to do?

(She brings the gun up slowly to point at his head.) . . .

Thought you wanted to live forever, Dirk? Well, here's how. . . .

I'm not going to kill *myself.* That'll happen soon enough. No. I'm going to ride the wave of my notoriety for the last few months. I'll be up there with all the other celebrity assassins, except special because I'm English and female. Even better. I don't have to feel too bad about it, because I'll know that I have removed from the planet a completely superfluous person who would otherwise have spent his dotage abusing unearned power. . . .

You'll get to live fast, die comparatively young and leave a pretty corpse. I mean, there's only so many face-lifts a man can have before he has to start shaving behind his ears, am I right?

(Pause.)

Thought so. You haven't got long, Dirk, before you're a joke. You'll never be a grand old man of the screen or the Senate — you haven't got the talent, and you're losing the looks. You left acting at the top of your career — that was wise, but it's all downhill from here. The rest of your life will be lived out in public and the world will watch you shrink and fade. They'll watch you sag and wrinkle; they'll see your eyes glaze over and your hands tremble and little by little the image of you when you were young will fade away. You'll kill your own legend by living too long. Think Marilyn, Elvis, Bogart: dying young is the thing! You're almost out of the zone. I can promise you, after this you'll have untouchable cultural icon status — maybe not along the lines of Diana, but you never actually tortured puppies so I'm guessing canonization *à la* John Lennon or James Dean. It's pretty much win-win, really. . . .

What have I got to lose?

HELEN'S MOST FAVORITE DAY
Mark Dunn

Comic
Ruta, forty-two

Ruta is asking a coy man named Herman if he loves her.

RUTA: Now, I know this is *not* the reason I invited you over here, Herman. But this afternoon, watching you sitting at your tidy little desk, drudging through your daily routine — then taking your 3:30 coffee break — at precisely 3:30 — not 3:31, mind you — never, no God forbid, 3:29. Enslaved to "same, same, same, same, same." And later when Helen came home and congratulated me on getting that embarrassingly measly honorable mention. For something I put all my heart and soul into. Like the way I've put my heart and soul into hoping against hope that you'd some day get up from your desk and walk over to *my* desk for a change, for a nice, refreshing change — not at 3:30, not even at 3:35, Herman, but at 3:47 — no, 3:47 and a half! — and say to me, "Ruta, dear, I have an idea: let's go sit in the park. You and me — just the two of us, Ruta. Let's us park it in the park and get ourselves drunk on — on — *Woodsman's Axes!*" Thinking on all that, dearest Herman, has given me the courage — . . .

Oh Herman, just shut up and listen. I'm talking about doing something other than sneaking me little gifts while my back is turned — something significant, Herman, to show me how you feel about me. Before it's over. Before we reach the end of our lives and we have nothing to show for it but lost chances. Look at me, Herman. Do you love me or not?

HOW I GOT THAT PART
Robert Pridham

Seriocomic
Beth, ten to fourteen

Auditioning for a part in the middle school play is a do-or-die mat-
ter for one group of girls. Here, Beth reveals her ongoing battle with
stage fright.

STAGE FRIGHT

BETH: I don't know how any of this happened. My being here, I mean.
I don't want to be in the play. Actually, I'd rather do almost anything
else you can think of than be in the play. Standing out there on the
stage? In front of all those people? *(She shudders.)* I think I'm just here
because everyone else is here. It's like mass hysteria or something.
Everyone's trying to be in the play, they're all shouting and pushing
so I just run right along with them because it seems like the right
thing to do, right? I mean, I don't want to be left out or anything.
My mother says: "Beth honey, the play is coming up soon and I hope
you'll try out because you could really use a boost to your self-
confidence!" What's wrong with my self-confidence? I don't have anything wrong with my self-confidence. I'm just quiet, that's all. The
only thing wrong with my self-confidence is that my mother keeps
worrying that there's something wrong with my self-confidence.
"I remember my first play," she says, "and I remember how wonderful it was to be up there in front of all those people! Just wonderful!"
Wonderful? Hah! You're standing up there in the dark worrying that
you'll forget your lines or sing the wrong note or fall off the edge of
the stage. And now here I am, standing up on the stage, and the director is saying: "Alright, I want big, big voices and lots of feeling!"
And my palms are all sweaty and my knees are shaking and I can't

get my mouth to open and my tongue won't work and I can't breathe and I'm starting to see spots in front of my eyes and I'm pretty sure I'm going to be dead in about three seconds.

What's so wonderful about that?

HOW I GOT THAT PART
Robert Pridham

Comic
Tyra, ten to fourteen

*Auditioning for a part in the middle school play is a do-or-die
matter for one group of girls. Here, Tyra tells us how she prepares
for her big opening night.*

BIT PART

TYRA: There are no small parts, only small actors. That's what my father
always says. And that's what he said when I told him I was going to
be "The Third Woman Who Sits Under the Toadstool," even though
I really wanted to be "The Second Woman Who Waits by the Wishing Well." See, the second woman is a much bigger part. Well, not
MUCH bigger, but she gets to have a whole scene with the princess,
which is about fifteen whole lines, and "The Third Woman Who Sits
Under the Toadstool" only says one word: BEWARE! That's all she
says: BEWARE! I mean, you'd think they could figure out something
else for her to say: LOOK OUT! Maybe, or even WATCH OUT BE-
HIND YOU! Or even DON'T TURN AROUND OR YOU'LL SEE
THE WORST THING YOU'VE EVER SEEN IN YOUR LIFE! My
father says that everyone has to start someplace. He says that even
Dustin Hoffman started out by playing parts with only one or two
lines, and Dustin Hoffman never complained. Dustin Hoffman just
went out there and did it. So I start thinking about my line. I mean,
if I only get to say one word, I might as well make sure it's going to
be the one word everyone remembers. So I practice:

(A threatening voice.) BEWARE! *(A different voice.)* BEWARE!
(Still another voice.) BEWARE!

*I practice with arm gestures: BEWARE! I practice with a scarf over
my head: BEWARE! (She is really getting into it now, trying out as many*

different voices as she can muster.) I practice under the bed, like I'm under the toadstool: BEWARE! I practice with all of the lights out in my room, to get into the mood: BEWARE! BEWARE! BEWARE! BEWARE! I spend weeks getting it just right. I mean, I'm really getting good at it! It may be only one word, but it's gonna be the one word nobody ever forgets! Who cares about the princess! Who cares about the second woman and her dumb old wishing well. The star of this play is definitely gonna be "THE THIRD WOMAN WHO SITS UNDER THE TOAD-STOOL!!!"

I just have one question: Who the heck is Dustin Hoffman?

HOW I GOT THAT PART
Robert Pridham

Comic
Amber, ten to fourteen

> *Auditioning for a part in the middle school play is a do-or-die*
> *matter for one group of girls. Here, Amber talks about the night-*
> *mare of auditioning in front of her classmates.*

AUDITIONS

AMBER: Auditions. The worst word in the English language. You think the word EXAM is bad? Hah. At least with an exam you can flop in the privacy of your own mind. But with an audition, there's no place to hide. Good morning, I'm Amber Pearl, and I'm here today to humiliate and embarrass myself in the most public way possible by doing whatever you tell me to do, no matter how stupid I feel doing it, in front of anybody who happens to be sitting out there. Of course, I have no idea what kind of actress you're looking for, but I'm pretty sure it's not me. But please — sit back, get comfortable, and watch in amazement as this innocent young girl, who never wished harm on anyone else in her life, who's always been friendly to animals and recycles all of her plastic to help save the environment, becomes a source of never-ending humor for her classmates. *(She assumes the different voices and attitudes of her classmates.)* "Did you see what Amber did for her audition?" "Omigosh what a jerk!" "What was she thinking?" "She can't sing!" "She can't act!" "What made her think she could try out in the first place?" "Back to plumbing school!" Yup, that's me! The *Titanic!* The Hindenburg! The San Francisco Earthquake! The whole city of Chicago just before that cow kicks over the lantern! I'm the biggest disaster in the history of the world!

Just watch me shine!!!!!

HOW I GOT THAT PART
Robert Pridham

Comic
Annie, ten to fourteen

> *Auditioning for a part in the middle school play is a do-or-die
> experience for one group of girls. Here, Annie tells us what's wrong
> with the audition process — and how we should fix it.*

CHORUS LINE

ANNIE: When I was in the fifth grade, my mother took me to see this play
at the little theater in the town where I live. It was called *A Chorus
Line* and that's just what it was all about. A chorus line. Being in one,
I mean. See, there are all these actors and actresses trying to get a part
in this show — they never tell you what show it is, it's just "the
show" — and it's really, really important for them to get parts in it.
I mean, they'll do just about anything to be in it. And there's this director — he's a character in the play, I mean a character in *A Chorus
Line,* not a character in the show they're trying to do in *A Chorus
Line* — and he's out in back of the audience in the dark, and he's
telling these actors who are trying out that they aren't good enough
to be in the show, you know, like "You can't act, get off the stage!"
or "You, you can't sing, get off the stage!" And he keeps waiting for
somebody better to come along or they're not going to be able to do
the show at all, but he's got all these actors and actresses who will do
anything to get a part and if somebody better doesn't come along,
then they're all he's got. And he makes them dance until they practically fall down they're so tired, and a couple of them start crying
because it's like the end of the world if they don't get in this show.
And after all that, at the very end, the whole chorus comes march-
ing out — and they're ALL in it! Everybody who tried out! Everybody gets a part! And they're all in gold with top hats and they're all

singing. My mom said it was because they didn't have enough actors to play the parts of the actors who don't get parts. But I don't think so.

What I think is that ALL plays should be like that. Everybody who tries out should get a part. Everybody gets to sing and dance and act. And wear a gold top hat!

IDA LUPINO IN THE DARK
Don Nigro

Seriocomic
Minnie, twenties

Minnie is a young woman who's slowly losing her mind. She pro-
tects herself by retreating into a strange private world in which she
sits in the dark and imagines that she is the film star and pioneer-
ing woman director Ida Lupino, making her own weird black-and-
white movies in her head.

MINNIE: Sydney Greenstreet sweats under the rotating ceiling fan, suck-
ing on his hookah, while in the twisted labyrinth of Paris, Peter Lorre
is being chased by a severed hand. Sam Spade pours himself another
Scotch as we flash back to Ingrid Bergman weeping in the gazebo
while Cary Grant creeps through the moonlit bedroom window and
Paganini's violin wails like a demon lover. Suddenly a huge black raven
flaps in the window. CAWWW CAWWW CAWWW. You can hear
the film cricketing through the sprockets. Boston Blackie lights his
cigar, and we see revealed the face of Veronica Lake, but Conrad Veidt
is lurking like a preying mantis in the cobbled alleyway. He is a Nazi
vampire golem, the zombie servant of Bela Lugosi. Then, in the distance, we hear the sound of a lonely fog horn. It's Spencer Tracy, home
from King Solomon's Mines. Scrub the poop deck, Long John! cries
Tugboat Annie. All ashore that's going ashore. It's New York in the
forties, but they've all met before, in Morocco. Bogie has nightmares
in which he sees these ceiling fans spinning forever. He got a touch
of malaria from Shanghai Lil on the road to Mandalay. Gray rain drips
off the brim of Orson Welles' hat, in the sewers under Grand Cen-
tral Station. Quiet, my little babushka. No one can be trusted in Tang-
iers. There are Nazi spies everywhere. Claude Rains is invisible. There's
a microphone hidden in Adolph Menjou's mustache. The Marx Broth-
ers are running through the Grand Hotel, past Buster Keaton, who's

sharing a corned beef sandwich with Francis the Talking Mule. They've got to win back the circus for Maureen O'Sullivan in the big horse race at the Bowery. Would you please shut the door? I'm trying to work in here. Places for the big waterfall number. Virgins on the right. Quiet on the set. OK. Roll 'em. The fog rolls in over Baker Street. Marlene Dietrich wants to hire Philip Marlowe, who keeps getting phone calls from Erich von Stroheim, who's dead. Ann Sothern is his wise-cracking secretary. Meanwhile, in the dark house in the country, George Brent is trying to drive Merle Oberon insane. He's strangled Rhonda Fleming under the spiral staircase. Boris Karloff is burying ZaSu Pitts in the garden while Lon Chaney fingers his organ in the subterranean catacombs. His son Larry turns to a wolf when the wolfbane blooms, and at the gypsy caravan, Aquanetta has the bumps on her read by Marya Ouspenskaya, who gazes deep into her crystal monkey and warns her to beware of George Zucco. As the rain falls on Castle Frankenstein, Charlie Chan arrives. Great Scott, Watson, what a fool I've been! Pray God we may not be too late!

IN THE CONTINUUM
Danai Gurira and Nikkole Salter

Seriocomic
Petronella, African, could be any age, thirties to fifties

> In the Continuum *deals with AIDS as it affects African and African-American women. Petronella is a well-to-do woman who works in support of various causes.*

PETRONELLA: . . . oh you got those here? They look just look just like the Stella McCartney pumps I bought at Harrods. I actually know her personally, she gave me a pair — she couldn't give them to her step-mother — she only has one leg! Did you say you worked ZBC? Oh, *(Laughs.)* no, I am sorry, I just got back home so I am still adjusting to all the lingo, someone the other day called it Dead BC. Good for you though hey! You were always a great public speaker! Careful Love-more! God, the way people drive in this country! In England he would have been arrested on the spot! Me, oh, well . . . I went abroad soon after high school, to study at London School of Economics, I was there for both my undergrad and my masters, International Relations with a focus on Human Rights and Gender Development, and I am still there mostly, I work as a consultant for big organizations, the UN, OXFAM, stuff like that. Right now, I have been really focused on HIV and Southern African women and of course all the big organizations abroad are going to hire me right? Perfect poster child — but I can't complain, I've been working with DATA — Debt, AIDS, Trade, Africa — Bono — he's a rock star — has an organization, they fly me everywhere, I do the research, tell them how to help, where to spend their money — so now I am home for a moment. And home is so sad hey, it's breaking my heart!! And on one wants to give Zim anything hey! Global Fund, UN, and we need it so badly, even though they are manufacturing some drugs here, they are not the best kind and how is anyone supposed to find the money to pay for them long term? In this economy?!! It's a mess. And where does one begin to try and help? . . .

. . . there is not even any bloody petrol! This is NOT the country we grew up! How do you survive? anyway, concerning the whole AIDS issue — I'm actually trying to get some statistics — that's why I was at the clinic — naturally the head nurse was on a two hour lunch or something! Zimboes! I don't know what sort of records these clinics even keep — I'm trying to find out how many expecting mothers test positive — I am almost scared to hear — just bloody heartbreaking. And you know, I am really beginning to wonder about Western solutions in general, how much can they really help us? They don't know us!! And we always look to them as our source of hope and redemption! We've been programmed! Ever since school man, do you remember how we loved to study like the Jonathan Swifts and the bloody Jane Austens!!! What did we have to do with their bloody worlds! But we loved it and looked down at our own stuff! I have since read Chinua Achebe, Yvonne Vera, people like that! They are amazing, our OWN stuff. And this music! Lovemore — turn that down! We have our own hip-hop, but most if it sounds like they're trying to be bloody American! It's the same with this, I am telling you, we have the answers and we don't know it. I have been thinking a lot about our own traditional AFRICAN healing. I am not saying they have the cures or whatever, but there is something in it, you can't argue that. Remember Sisi Thembi? . . .

. . . she was such a mad mad, MAD, woman, I can't believe she is in the church now! Oh what a shame — remember how she swore by witch doctors? Remember how her daughter had some sickness no one could figure out — she said her witch doctor — sorry — traditional healer — fixed it! She had to do some strange things but it worked and nothing else did. There is something to it I tell you. Oh, wooah, what are you doing the car is still moving. *(Getting out of car, yelling.)* You work for ZBC — do you host that show *Breaking New Ground?* I really want to be on it, I think I have a lot to say that the country needs to hear, I am breaking new bloody ground . . .

IN THE CONTINUUM
Danai Gurira and Nikkole Salter

Seriocomic
Sex Worker, could be any age.

This character is an African prostitute, talking to an old high school chum, who has asked her advice. She enters smoking.

SEX WORKER: Dahling, dahling, dahling. How the bloody hell am I supposed to know how to make a man fall asleep so you can put a n'yanga's potion on his penis? Don't believe those stories about prostitutes stealing the penises of men who don't pay. It's bullshit! Wish it wasn't. *(Starts to sit, gets back up.)* Just give a second my dahling. *(Gets some tissue, wipes between her legs.)* What a messy bastard. *(Sits.)* Right, shit, you've got yourself into a pot of poo my girl. Who would have thought Miss Priss Abigail would get herself in such a bind! Let me help you out my sister, since you have come to your old high school chum for advice. You have to face the truth. Your marriage is ova. You think you make him stay? You know how these men are! He will blame you for everything, even though you got it from him. And the in-laws! Do you remember Elizabeth Chidzero? It happened to her! Sent back to her village, penniless, the kids taken by the bastard and his family, even though she got it from him! Now she is waking up to the cockerels singing "kokoriko" — dancing at those fucking village pungwes for those old farts and washing in the river, while she's sick as a bloody dog! You think it won't happen to you? You'll find yourself back in your village, grinding corn singing dum dum duri, dum dum duri. Ha, and you were always the one who was going to go to America or something and become rich and famous. What did you say your man's name was again? AHHHH *(Deep in thought, then looks back at Abigail.)* All I'll say is I am not surprised. Shame. The best thing I can offer you my sister is a new lifestyle. Leave the bastard. He gave you AIDS! I can hook you up with a nice beneficiary who will take such good care of you my love, you will never need that man of your again. He will give you enough cash get the medicine, save your baby! It's nicer to feel a beautiful piece of life pushing out of you than a dead piece of flesh coming inside you. You can take your son stay in your own place. Take care of the man every now and then. Get the doughs, buy the drugs. And you will live so much longer futi. And no bullshit in-law stress. What have you got to lose my dahling? You think this lifestyle is planned? The economy is shit, my dear. I was a secretary, couldn't pay for my rent, couldn't pay for my electric, couldn't pay for my DSTV! And I was *not* going back to watching Dead BC. No offense. So I did it once, did it twice, next thing you know I had a business. Listen, there is *nothing* wrong with being a kept woman, it's the least these bastards can do for us. And these Africa men, they love to flex their dollars, makes their dicks hard. So, it's there for the taking. You have to decide what's more important to you. Remain Miss Priss Abigail, or become a survivor because you can't save both your marriage and that baby. You can keep quiet about it, act as if nothing is wrong and die horribly — watching your kid die too, all because you wanted to remain the perfect little shona wife. Which many have done. Or you can take care of yourself and your child. Personally, I want to be a mother. I have this one guy, he's a client, a really nice guy hey! He wants me to have his baby. He say, no condoms. Saka, me I say why not! It's important to be a mother, it's the one thing we can do that these bastards can't! This is just a hope for me, but you, you have children, so be a mother. And forget about that potion girlie. Those n'yangas are mad. If they had anything that worked, Africa wouldn't even have AIDS. *(Looks outside.)* Shit! Sorry beby, a new customer — this one needs a little bit more time. One of those old government chef bastards. The machinery takes a little longer to oil. Abi, Abigail — you have to do something, you can't keep running around like Speedy Gonzales! It's the best offer you are going to get! *(Puts out cigarette, straightens out wig and shirt, looks over at client approaching.)* Hi, howzit!?

IN THE CONTINUUM
Danai Gurira and Nikkole Salter

Dramatic
Mama, African, thirties to forties

> In the Continuum *is a play that deals with AIDS among African
> and African-American women. Here, Mama is chastising her daugh-
> ter. (* = Imani, six-month-old baby, crying.)*

MAMA: *Hey! Hey!! Get offa my grass! Get offa my grass and take your
Funyion bag with you. *(To herself.)* Bad ass kids. *(Beat.)* *Well, well,
well. I knew you'd come back. Lemme guess: They didn't believe your
lies about the Good Shepherd either? You thought it was gon' be easy
as that. Well, life is not easy, guess you have to learn the hard way.
And now you wanna come back. I'm still goin' to family court off of
the shit you pulled; anger management, freakin' parenting classes like
I don't know what the hell I'm doin', and you wanna come back just
like that? No apology, no nothin'? And then you got the nerve to ask
me for $400 — how you gon' pay me back? You got a job? You look
like a damn prostitute, what are you wearin'? It's nine o'clock in the
morning, walkin' 'round like you been walkin' the streets.

(Seriously.) Is you walkin' the streets, Nia?

Don't get smart with me!

Then what you need $400 for, huh? Probably some Guess jeans.
What happened to the money from your poetry contest? Ain't nobody payin' you to put'ch'a little rhymes together no more? Ain't got
no job, no place to live, but spend all yo' time writin' poetry and shop-
pin' — for $400 Guess jeans. Are they self-cleaning? Do they pay rent?
If anybody's gettin' $400 'round here, *'guess'* who it's gonna be — ME.
I'm tired of comin' second to ya'll. I can't remember the last time I
had me some lotion or some new panties. Besides, you grown, remember? And us grown folk, we pay for our own shit. You old enough.
Hell, when I was nineteen I was * — And don't think you slick goin'

behind my back askin' Marvin for the money. I thought you didn't like him. He ain'tcha daddy, so stop askin' him fo' shit. *(To Imani.)* Huh? He's yo' daddy, huh? Yo' daddy! *(To Nia.)* You should ask that lil' boyfriend of yours, Darnell, for $400. He'll buy them pants for you . . . since he the one like to get in 'em so often. Don't think I didn't usta hear your little narrow behind climbin' out the window to go oochie coochie with that boy. Like you the first one discovered how to sneak out the house. I invented that shit. I already been everywhere you been, Nia. And I was just tryin' to keep your fast ass from goin' to half of them places. OH! But you grown! Well, I'ma tell yo' grown ass this: I know you like him, and he look like he goin' places,* but don't end up pregnant, Nia. Cuz once you turn this switch on, you can't turn it off, and I'ma damned if I end up raisin' your kids cuz you couldn't use a condom. Oh, OH! *(To Imani.)* She woman enough to do that, but she can't talk the talk. *(To Nia.)* What would you rather I say, Ms. Nia? Strap on the jimmy? Pull the balloon over the sausage? Please, I wish somebody had told me about this shit, half-a ya'll wouldn't be here. And now days, you can catch all kinda stuff. Stuff you can't get rid of cuz it gets in your blood. Trust me: three minutes of slappin' bellies ain't worth death. And that's what it is, death. * What? It's a government experiment. They've done it before and will do it again. You think it's consequential that we the ones got it the most out of everybody. They been tryin' to get rid of us since the Emancipation. First they lynched us, then they got us high so they could put us in prison. Then they got the ones that ain't incarcerated to shoot up each other and now they brought this hopin' that we fuck ourselves to death. And you know they got a cure. What you think the whole civilian rights was about? That's why they really assassinated Martin: to distract us from the monkey fuckers that brought it back from Africa to kill us. And they killed Malcolm cuz, on his pilgrimage, he found out who the monkey fuckers were. You got to know your history. It's outta control —

I know, I know, you love Darnell. Darnell love you. Ya'll invincible in love. Yes, I know. I was in love too. Five times. Remember that. All I had to worry about was gettin' pregnant, but you got a whole slew of other stuff to think about. Real love last forever, but so do real mistakes.

(To Imani.) Yes, they do, huh? Yes they do! And I'ma tell you, just like I tol' them, yes I am, yes I am! You only got me 'til you're eighteen. That's it! * *(To Nia.)* That's it. Now you can go on in the back and get $60 outta my purse so that you can get a room to rent for the night, cuz you can't stay here. I ain't gonna let ya'll run my world forever. You grown, remember. And I ain't gonna let you scare this man away. Uh, uh. One down four to go.

Look at them. Hey! HEY! Stop sprayin' paint on them walls, that shit ain't art.* *(She exits.)*

IN THE CONTINUUM
Danai Gurira and Nikkole Salter

Dramatic
Nia, late teens, early twenties

> *Nia, a young African-American woman, is pregnant by a future pro basketball star, who has given her a check for $5,000 to get the matter taken care of and then to go away. Here, she is talking to her unborn child.*

NIA: *(Drunk.)* It smell like booty. I wish I could fly away. Dirty-ass motel. Guess what baby. Guess what? *(Dumping her purse.)* Today your mommy opened her purse to see how much money she had and she had a five dollar bill and a $5,000 check. $5,000. *(Folding up the check and putting it aside.)* No, baby, we don't need his money. No, we don't! Mommy will go tomorrow and see if they still want her at Nordstrom. What was they payin'? Five dollars. No baby, no, we can do it. Come on, I'ma show you. We just have to budget. *(Tearing a piece of the five dollar bill with each item.)* This, this right here is for my retirement fund. Cuz Oprah says you should pay yourself first. This, this is for your college fund, cuz you going to college. This for rent . . . on our mansion in Beverly Hills. And my Mercedes. What else? What else you want baby? Oh yeah. Gas, water, and lights. That's it. That the life right there, baby. You got, retirement, college, mansion, Mercedes, gas, water, lights. Yeah! Ooooo! Mommy forgot to put food in the budget! How mommy forget about the food? But there's no more money. $5,000. *(She breaks down in tears.)* He knew! He knew! And he knows you're his baby cuz he the one made me pregnant. And she thinks she can throw $5,000 at me and I'ma just be quiet? $5,000 dollars. I sold myself for $5,000. That's how much I cost. No baby, that's how much you cost. *(Balling up the check and throwing it down.)* No, no, we don't need his money. This is what we gonna do, baby. *(Picking up the pieces of the five dollar bill.)* We'll make the light money the food money. Cuz we gotta eat, but we don't need no lights. We don't need no lights let the muthafuckas burn! *(She b-boxes and makes a beat on the furniture.)* Come on, baby. Cuz we got, what we got? What we got!? Huh? We got, we got

Sunlight

Insight

Out of sight — out of mind.

JIMMY CARTER WAS A DEMOCRAT

Rinne Groff

Dramatic
Emily, twenties to thirties

> *Hoping for a better, more secure life with her new boyfriend, Emily
> has given up her political activities with the air traffic controllers'
> union, quit her job in the control tower and ended a long affair
> with a married coworker. She knows that her old life was giving
> her nothing but ulcers, but she still misses the rush it gave her.*

EMILY: There's a lot of pressure, a lot of pressures, a lot of forces that con-
spire to keep us down.

Gravity is the worst, of all those forces. You can't get away from
it. Gravity's always there. It dooms us straight from the start. I read
somewhere that when a woman gets pregnant, you know egg and
sperm, right away that little package starts turning and stuff, and it's
all affected by gravity. I mean, even before we know who we are, even
before we're born; this shit, it's just pulling on us. It colors everything.
What's the first thing that pops into your head when you hear these
words: Up? High? She's flying? Those ought to be nice words, great
words, words of potential. But on account of gravity, all you can think
of is the inevitable Down; Low; She's crashed.

But then there's airplanes, right? And you watch them and you
think they've really got it figured out. When a plane's taking off and
there it goes gliding upwards, or if you're riding in one of those new
jets, so smooth, if you have a good pilot, you could maybe forget about
your morbid visions of tailpipes in flames and really believe, believe
for a moment that you can overcome . . . fuck, you could overcome
anything, you're flying, you did it.

Why can't that be the way we think? Why can't we teach our children that in the womb? Not to be afraid. Not to assume yeah, sure

you're Up now, but here comes Failure, you might as well throw in the towel. And if a baby could feel all right, up in the air, in a plane, soaring along, could experience freedom from all that pulls her down; if she could learn that, can't you maybe imagine that she could get free of a bunch of other shit, too? That we'd grow as a species and triumph? And change, and growth, and all that are possible?

She's flying. She's flying.

MEDEA
Joseph Goodrich

Dramatic
Medea, twenties to thirties

> *Against his better judgment, Creon has agreed to let the banished*
> *Medea stay in Corinth for another day. Here, Medea figures out how*
> *she will use that day to bring about the destruction of her husband,*
> *Jason, and his new love, who is Creon's daughter.*

MEDEA: The game's not over yet. Far from it. If Creon and Jason and his
woman think they're safe, they'd better think again. You saw the way
I begged and pleaded, how I clutched his sleeve and cried? I humil-
iated myself: That was the price of another day in Corinth. I paid it,
though — even if it made me want to vomit just to touch him . . .
He gave me a day. He'll live just long enough to wish he hadn't. And
then he'll join his daughter and my husband in the grave. I'll make
sure of that . . .

    The question now is, how will I do it? So many roads lead to
the same destination . . . Should I burn the palace down? Or sneak
into their bedroom, catch them in the act and hack away at tender
flesh, stab and slice until I blunt the knife on bone?

    No. I might get caught before I've had the time to act. The palace
guards would kill me on the spot — but not before they'd forced me
down and raped me, laughing as I cried, laughing at Medea, that stupid fucking bitch who thought she'd . . .

    No.

    Poison.

    Of course.

    Poison is the way.

    I'm going to do it. I'm actually going to do it. I'm actually going
to do it . . .

    What'll happen next — where I'll go, who will take me in —

I don't know. I may find out that what I've always feared the most, something I've always suspected, just might be true: That there is no home on earth for me at all. That I really might be as lonely as I feel. That I've always been alone, and always will be.

Well — if it's true, it's true.

I'll wrap my cloak about me and shiver in the sun.

But if there is a refuge, some shelter for me somewhere, then poison is my choice. And when they're dead, I'll slip away as softly as the death I've brought.

If not, I'll take my chances with the knife,

And give my life to see theirs ended.

Hecate,

Goddess of Night, Queen of the Moon, I swear it:

Those who hurt Medea are hurt by her in turn.

I swear it.

Now, Medea, make your plans.

You know what to do. Now you must do it.

Practice the woman's art, deception.

Bring them destruction.

Give them instruction in how

To die the way you've lived:

In torment.

MEDEA
Joseph Goodrich

Dramatic
Medea, twenties to thirties

*Medea counters Jason's very smooth and logical reasons for leaving
her for another woman with a blast of what she believes to be the
blunt and brutal truth of the matter.*

MEDEA: After what you've done
You have the gall to show up here
And say all that to me?
You hypocrite.
You spit in my face and tell me
I'm beautiful?
You murder our love, then offer
To pay for the funeral?
Is that the way an honorable man behaves?
I'm glad you're here, though in a way.
It gives me the chance to make you hear
The truth.
You've heard of it, the truth? It's like a
Woman's love: Undeniable, absolute, durable
As iron but shattered by a single lie.
When you were looking for the golden fleece,
Who killed the serpent wrapped around
The treasure? Anyone on board the Argo
At the time will tell you it was me.
Who wrapped himself in glory
When the fleece was found?
That was you.
Who murdered Pelias, who butchered
The old king and made sure his

Daughters got the blame?
Who left the home she loved,
Who tore apart her family,
Who threw her past away
In the madness of a moment?
Who has blood on her hands
And on her conscious?
Me.
Medea did.
Medea has.
Who was all this done for?
Who was I trying to please?
One man, and one man only:
You.
You, Jason.
Jason.
Jason.
Jason.
Jason.
Only you.
Whose love justified the butchery,
The damage and destruction?
Yours.
Your love . . . for me.
It's strange:
I thought I'd served you well.
I killed for you, I gave you children.
Two beautiful boys, Jason.
Or have you forgotten that?
You seem to have forgotten so much
Lately . . .
I'll ask you again as if I didn't
Know the answer in advance:
Honor the bonds that bind us.
Prove to me your word is good.
Take this hand and swear to me

You'll keep the promises you made
When I set out on this course with you.
. . . No?
Once you were happy to hold these hands.
You pressed your lips on mine.
You kissed these breasts.
I felt your hot breath on my neck,
My belly, my cunt . . .
You said I was your world. You said that.
You said so many things when we were close . . .
Tell me something now.
Pretend, for a moment, that you're my friend.
Tell me what to do. Advise me. I can't go home
And I can't stay here. By helping you I hurt
Myself: No one wants me, no one will have me,
No one will give me a place to rest. True, I
Was rewarded for my help — a husband. A home,
A future without worry, doubt or fear.
I hope your new wife is half as lucky.
She'll have to be.
In the world of things, what's true is easily
Distinguished from what's false. Fool's gold
Is just a stone. A diamond scratches glass.
Sandstone crumbles in your hand. But a man
Who lies with every breath looks just the same
As one you'd trust your life with . . . Until he
Snaps your neck in the middle of a kiss.

MEDEA
Joseph Goodrich

Dramatic
Medea, twenties to thirties

> *Medea professes her delight at Jason's plans to take up with another*
> *woman, and she begs his forgiveness for standing in the way. But*
> *her delight is feigned, and her real intentions are murderous.*

MEDEA: Jason . . . My dear, dear Jason . . . You've always been so good at
understanding me. You forgive my rages, my fits of emotion because
we've shared so much together in the past. I'm asking you to understand again, and forgive me. I've been thinking it over and I see
how . . . unwisely I've behaved. All you've been trying to do is help
me — me and the children — and all I can do is . . . Well, it's like
you said: I really am my own worst enemy. Who am I to question
how the Gods arrange our lives? Especially when it's not just me who's
involved, but our children, too. You were thinking ahead; I was cling-
ing to the past. I've been a foolish, stupid, stubborn woman, and I
admit it. I think the alliance you've arranged is wonderful — for you,
for the children, for me — and I'm sorry I haven't played a bigger
part in it. If I'd only been reasonable, right now I'd be laughing with
the bride-to-be, sharing little secrets . . . indulging in the pleasures
that surround a wedding . . . There's no need to torture myself with
all that might-have-been. It's enough to say I'm sorry. You could have
shown a little better sense, though — you don't mind if I say this,
do you? — a little better sense when I flew off the handle. That's how
women are. They get upset and lose perspective. We rely on men for
the reason and balance and wisdom we just don't have. But I can't be
angry with you for that. This has been a difficult time for you, too.
And all I did was make it worse. Forgive me . . . Can you do
that? . . . Children! Where are you? Children!

　　There you are. There's my darlings. Come over here, please . . .

Now: give your father a hug . . . that's right. Your mommy and daddy have had a nice long talk, and we're not angry at each other anymore. You've been brave little soldiers, but everything's fine now. Everything's fine. We're all very happy and . . .

(She begins to cry.)

. . . I'm sorry. I was just thinking of what the future holds for the innocent . . . Don't pay any attention to me . . . It's silly — everything's fine now, and I can't . . . Hold them tight, Jason. Hold them tight . . . Oh . . . Oh . . .

NEVER TELL
James Christy

Dramatic
Liz, fourteen

> *Liz is quiet, troubled, introverted. The character is in her late*
> *twenties during the course of the play, but in this monologue she is*
> *fourteen. She speaks directly to the audience.*

LIZ: It was last summer. My dad had a birthday party for my mom and
her brother Sam came. Uncle Sam. When he'd see us, he'd point his
finger at us and yell out "I want you" and give us these painful bear
hugs. So he was drinking bourbon and telling us this story about this
guy who used to work with him at his shop. Every Friday they'd go
to this local bar and have beers with their lunch. So one day the guy
got really drunk, and when they got back my uncle told him he should
be careful 'cause they work with all this heavy machinery. And the
guy laughs and says he's fine. And like five minutes later the guy slices
off three of his fingers. He was so drunk he said it didn't even hurt,
he just felt warm blood on his hands. On the way to the hospital he
was holding up his middle finger and pointing it at my uncle and
laughing. It was kinda sad 'cause he got fired and didn't even get
worker's comp because he was drunk and all. But the way Uncle Sam
told it it was so funny.

(*Beat.*)

I went up to bed but I could still hear him and my mom as I
watched a movie in my room. John Cusack was talking to some girl,
I fell half-asleep and started dreaming that he was talking to me. And
in the dream he was looking at me and saying something and it was
perfect, you know? Right then I looked up and my Uncle Sam was
in my room. He just stood there watching the John Cusack movie
for a long time. Then he asked me if I had a boyfriend and I said no.
And he said that was a shame because he thought I was pretty. I knew

he was drunk and I knew it wasn't right that he was in my room but it seemed like he meant it. And then he came into my bed. And I said that he should go but he told me I knew he wasn't going to go and I should be quiet. And when he was doing it I remember being surprised that I could still hear the movie. I thought it was supposed to be louder with grunting and stuff but I could still hear John Cusack like before. And when he was done he got up and put his hand on my hair and said it would be our secret. But he said it like he knew it already, he knew I wouldn't tell. And he was right, I haven't. And I won't.

99 HISTORIES
Julia Cho

Dramatic
Eunice, Korean-American, late twenties

> *Eunice is trying to decide what to do about an unwanted pregnancy.*
> *Here, she is writing a letter to her unborn child.*

EUNICE: Dear . . . whatsyourname.

To Whom It May Concern, I was your mother, no.

To . . . you.

To you.

I know you're hoping for some kind of epiphany or revelation. Well, I have nothing like that for you. The simple fact is, I was not made for you. That mother smell, that softness. I wasn't made for that. I was just a temp on Wall Street, a sad-faced, pale little office worker like Bartleby the Scrivener, looking out a window that faced only a wall. Speaking of which, optional reading list, books I like: *Bartleby the Scrivener,* Melville.

As to where you come from . . . well, there isn't much to tell. I come from a family that doesn't really talk about the past. For instance, my mother has a scar on her throat but I still don't know exactly how she got it. When I was a kid, I thought she said it was a "star," and so for most of my growing up, I thought she had some magic in her, right there, shaped like a mini-explosion.

I remember once, when I was in eighth grade, I had to make a family tree as a class project. *(Visual of a diagram with very few boxes and a lot of white space.)* Me. Only child. My father with two half-brothers I've never met. My father's parents, my mother's parents — grandfathers dead on both sides before I was even born. And that's it. Ta-Dah.

I took this chart to school, very proud of what I had done. And who was up first, but my best friend, Liz Grady. *(Visual of a diagram with boxes and lines branching out in wild proliferation.)* Her family tree was the size of a Volvo. She had people like Ann Boleyn, George Washington. Liz Grady oozed history. She once showed me the contents of her hope chest: linens from her grandmother, silver from her great-aunt, stuff that had been passed down for generations. I looked at it and thought to myself: I have no hope chest. I have no hope.

I'm just saying, so what if you grew up not knowing where you were from? Maybe more than hair color or eye shape, it's that feeling that proves you are mine.

99 HISTORIES
Julia Cho

Dramatic
Eunice, Korean-American, late twenties

> *Eunice is trying to decide what to do about an unwanted pregnancy.*
> *Here, she is writing a letter to her unborn child.*

EUNICE: My parents were old when they met. Old for their day and time.
He was thirty; she was twenty-nine. A year after they married, they
came here with nothing and opened and closed every kind of business you can think of. Liquor store, dry cleaning. And then they
opened a convenience store, open from eight to eleven, six days a week.
They worked together in that store for five years until the day my father was shot. My mother, to this day, has never talked about what
happened. Even though she was the one who called the ambulance
and sat with my father as he died. When I was in junior high, I saw
that famous film of Kennedy's assassination in history class. And ever
since then, in my head, when I think back on that day, I imagine my
father is Kennedy and my mom is Jacqueline. *(As Eunice talks, dim
lights come up on two vague figures dressed as Jacqueline and John F.
Kennedy. They are sitting as if in a car. They re-enact the shooting from
the Zapruder film, soundlessly, over and over again. Underneath the following, the sound of whispering begins to rise but it is impossible to make
out the words.)* When the bullet strikes him, he has no idea what has
happened. He is more surprised than in pain. When he falls over on
her, she screams over and over again. His blood stains her pink suit.
His blood stains her hands. And she will never be clean again.

PARADISE
Glyn O'Malley

Dramatic
Shoshana, forty-two

> *Shoshana is speaking to her newly arrived Israeli-American daughter Sarah about why she decided to move to a settlement in the West Bank outside Jerusalem.*

SHOSHANA: *(She can get up and wander as needed through this.)* Three summers ago as a prize, I took a couple of boys from my fifth grade class who I knew never got out of the city on a day trip to the beach. Good kids. Rough and tumble boys. We took a walk past where all the people were and over a little jetty where I used to look for crabs when I was a little girl. Above this jetty is an ancient little mosque that has been there forever. As the boys were playing in the water, and I was standing at the edge, I noticed a man come out of the mosque and stare at me. A young man — maybe, twenty. He laughed, and pointed at the boys, and came down the rocks to the beach, and over to me. He told me what fine sons I had, and I told him, no, they were not mine. I was a teacher, simply giving a present to some boys who could use one. He smiled. I asked him if it was a special day at the mosque, and he said, "No, it's very old. I wanted to see it and to pray." We were standing at the water's edge, and he suddenly drew a line in the sand with his toe. A line just in front of my feet where the waves were lapping. Then all of a sudden, his eyes turned very . . . intense . . . like light was coming out of them, and he said from his side of the line on the beach, "All of this is Palestine. Take your fine little Hebrew boys and leave. They will only come to ruin here. The tide has turned. Your day is over. We will drive you Jews back into the sea." Then he bowed slightly to me — very polite — walked away and got into a car and drove off. *(Beat.)* I was . . . speechless. Then every cell of blood in my body turned to ice. He was such a fine-looking young man . . . the light in his eyes . . . I realized that we had had a moment, just one small moment of talking across this "hard line" as you call it, and that if I ever met him again, he would kill me. That's when I decided I had to do something that would make a difference, and I moved here. . . .

Yes! Like we had our turn, our chance, our . . . little play at statehood. Our day can never be over, Sarah. Israel is not *only* an idea, it is a place again. The home to which every Jew's heart has been attached since Abraham had his sons. I won't go into the sea, and neither will you. If I have to stand on the other side of *his* hard line to keep it that way, then I will. Just know that I . . . *I* didn't put it there, or ever want it.

POODLE WITH GUITAR AND DARK GLASSES

Liz Duffy Adams

Seriocomic
Violet, twenties

Violet is a well-meaning, highly strung young woman in her twenties. She is sitting alone at a table with a telephone, notebook and pen. The phone rings; she picks up.

VIOLET: Neighborhood Action Help-line, this is Violet . . . Oh no, we don't do AIDS testing here, we're not a clinic. But I can give a referral . . . A number. I can give you a number to call. For a clinic. OK, the number is 634-2468. Ask for Sandy, she'll take care of you. OK. Good luck. *(She hangs up. Writes in notebook, murmuring:)* Woman, AIDS test referral, Sandy. *(The phone rings. She picks up.)*

Neighborhood Action Help-line, this is Violet. Oh, no, we don't do pregnancy tests, we're not a clinic. But I can give you the — hello? *(She hangs up. Writes in notebook:)* Pregnancy test, incomplete referral. *(Phone rings. She picks up.)* Neighborhood Action Hot-line, Violet. Oh, housing, yes, housing's tricky right now, there's a freeze on Section Eights, and there are hardly any low income units available in the neighborhood except for units being illegally warehoused. But I can give you a number to call. Ready? 899-3579, talk to Naomi, she can tell you where else to call. What? Oh. Oh no. No, I don't have any room in my apartment. I'm sor — Oh, I'm sure your kids are quiet and everything, I just, I'm sorry, I don't have room. It's a, it's a studio. I'm sorry but . . . Where are you now, in the . . . ? Oh, uh huh, the shelter. I know. I know. It's bad, I know. Look, you talk to Naomi. OK? You hang in there. Call me again if you want to talk about it. OK? OK. *(She hangs up. Starts to write in notebook but phone rings again.)*

Neighborhood Action Help-line, Violet. Oh, uh, por favor, slowly señora, mi espanol es no muy bueno. ¿Que? No comprendo. ¿Que? Oh, oh, OK. Neccessitas llamar ocho nueve nueve, tres cinco siete nueve, hablas a Naomi. Si. Si. ¿Que? Oh, no. No. No, mi casa es muy, um, poquita, yo no tengo . . . uh, lo siento, hablas a Naomi, ¿si? Si. No problema. Buen — Buenas noches. *(Hangs up. Phone rings. She picks up.)* Neighborhood Action Help-line, Violet . . . Hello? . . . Hello? . . . Is someone there? . . . Hello? . . . Can I help you? . . . Can I help you? . . . *(She hangs up. Phone rings. She picks up.)* Neighborhood Action Help-line, Violet . . . What? The birds are flying south? What do you mean? I don't understand. Hello? *(She hangs up. Writes in notebook:)*

Unidentifiable person, reporting bird migration. No referral. *(Phone rings. She answers.)* Neighborhood Action, the birds are flying south . . . I'm sorry, what? . . . Oh. I'm sorry, I can't help you. I have no number for you to call. I can't help you.

(She hangs up. Writes in notebook:) Man, asking about my underwear. No referral.

(Phone rings. She picks up.) Neighborhood, Violet, time to fly south. Don't call for help. Stock up on grubs. Fluff up and jettison your bone marrow. *(She hangs up. Phone rings. She picks up.)* A feather lands at my feet. I think about my mother. Long ago there was a fire and I became an orphan just like everybody else. Trajectory! Know your vector!

POODLE WITH GUITAR AND DARK GLASSES
Liz Duffy Adams

Dramatic
Fuchsia, twenties to thirties

> *Fuchsia DeMornay is an unromantic romance novelist in her*
> *twenties or thirties. her heroine has begun to behave wildly, despite*
> *Fuchsia's attempts to write to the usual formula. She is in her work*
> *studio, talking to her mysterious new neighbor Jerry. She speaks*
> *rapidly without even the slightest pause until the third-to-last line.*

FUCHSIA: I'm very confused, it's out of my hands, she's completely out of
control and where does that leave me? and you know romance used
to be so simple to me, just a meal ticket but suddenly everything's
being called into question, like can anyone explain to me the difference or boundary or link or dichotomy or what-have-you of love and
sex, you know, romance vs. lust, I mean is there an issue there or is
it just semantics or, you know, a matter of lighting: sharp focus is sex,
soft focus is romance? not useful distinctions maybe but you know
what do I know? haven't had sex in, Christ, years, mainly I suppose
because I'm JUST TERRIFIED, naturally; who are all these people
who are fucking as if it's HARMLESS, are they not paying attention?
and anyway I never can decide who it is, you know, who it is that I
desire, it feels like all or nothing, I mean like I could want AB-
SOLUTELY EVERYBODY, male, female, young, old, just the ut-
terly pansexual and have a carnal experience with every creature I
encounter or else shut it down and forget where I left the key, you
know, not even get started, because it's that middle ground where all
the distinctions have to be made, all those evaluations and choices,
that I personally find TOO MUCH. I don't know why I'm telling
you all this. I don't really know you. I don't know you at all. I hear
you're a photojournalist or something. I bet that's interesting. Snatch

65

yourself a hunk of what's happening and turn it into a paycheck. Or art. Which is photojournalism, money or art? I'm an orphan. I was separated from my family at a traveling fun fair and raised by kindly carneys. It was a good life. I have no regrets. I do sometimes wonder how I got here from there, you know what I mean? Like tonight. I was walking over here, around dusk. And I pass a couple screaming at each other on the sidewalk, just screaming in front of strangers and everything, and I'm kicking aside a discarded needle just as a couple of little kids run past me, playing, and it's all very comfortable and familiar in a way, the broken glass, the rubble-filled lots, the smell of sour wine as I pass a bar, and an ice cream truck comes cruising down the street, playing that little tune, you know? *(Imitates it.)* And I flashed on when I was a kid, in the carnival. Once in a while, if it started to rain, and there weren't any customers, the merry-go-round guys would keep it going for a while, and carneys who'd gotten caught in the rain away from their booths or trailers would jump on, you know, get out of the rain? And I'd be hanging onto my favorite horse, a really fierce black-maned stallion, and we'd be going around with the colored lights sparkling off the rain and the tinny old merry-go-round music playing and all those tough old carneys grinning and whooping except for the guys who were starting a card game in the swan-bench. *(Slight pause.)* I know there were a lot of steps in my life between then and now but for a moment I saw then and now side by side and it just did not make any sense at all.

POODLE WITH GUITAR AND DARK GLASSES

Liz Duffy Adams

Seriocomic
Jade, twenties to thirties

Jade is a hip young artist in her twenties or thirties. A dog portrait she's been commissioned to paint has cast her into a crisis of faith, as Blini the poodle has turned first into Elvis Presley and then into a more abstract icon. She speaks rapidly.

JADE: I was abandoned in a museum and raised by kindly museum guards. So you see I'm pretty much at home with art. We used to make the rounds at night and I'd look at the art by flashlight. I have a fierce grasp of detail. It's the bigger picture I have trouble with. My earliest art memories are of the bottoms of paintings, the lower edges. Because I was little, you know. I didn't understand what the signatures were for a long time. I couldn't read yet. I thought they were art too. I didn't quite get that people make art. I think I thought art was a natural phenomenon. Like I thought that the statues of gods in the classical wing were petrified people, people who were under a witch's spell or something. There was one I had a wicked crush on. One of those beautiful curly-haired athletes, lean marble body, sad empty eyes staring into the distance. Once at night I snuck out by myself with a flashlight, and climbed up onto his plinth, twining my tiny limbs around him, under the influence of some idiotic fairy tale. I kissed his cold, cold lips. No magical transformation. *(Slight pause.)* Life is so fucking disappointing. *(Slight pause.)* I don't know why I'm even talking to you. What does a photographer know about anything? Running around plagiarizing life and calling it art. Aaagh. Don't mind me. I'm just in a nasty funk 'cause I've been abandoned by my god. There's no reason for it, is there? You can see this paint brush in my hand, can't you? But there's the blank canvas. Blini has stopped talking to me. Why? Why? I don't know. I don't know anything anymore. I surrendered to the will of God or something and now it's left me twisting in the wind. I look at this object in my hand and it's a stranger to me. I can't use it and it's stopped using me. It's 3 A.M.; do you know where your raison d'être is? Yeah, yeah, yeah. What it boils down to, je suis fucked.

QUEEN MILLI OF GALT
Gary Kirkham

Dramatic
Milli, twenty-nine

Milli is expressing her feelings for Jonathan, an offstage character. This takes place in the 1920s.

MILLI: Jonathan? It's me. *(Pause.)* I think of you every day. The moment your train left the station, my heart presumed to imagine a story *(Pause.)* I imagined you crossed the ocean and arrived home to a cold angry girl whom you warmed with a smile. And right there, you proposed to her. You stumbled over your words. It was clumsy and silly and perfect. You surprised her. You always could surprise her. *(Pause.)* She wanted a small wedding. She filled the church with every single flower from the garden. She breathed in and never wanted to breathe out. On Sunday mornings you'd wake early and pick wildflowers that would wilt before finding their way into a vase. You let out a boyish laugh as she kissed your fingers that tasted of lavender. You put your ear to her belly and listened for a tiny heartbeat. You insisted on making "his" first toy. You turned a broken ironing board into a fine-looking rocking horse. She helped you with its mane. She used the wool from your old brown sweater. It smelled like . . . you. *(Pause.)* And when the sun went down you bundled up on the back porch. You drew her in close and in a warm whisper you boasted to the stars that you must be the happiest couple on earth. She forgave you for being "the war hero" . . . for being a little full of yourself. She forgave you for . . . almost . . . dying. *(Pause.)*

ROMEO TO GO
Jonathan Rand

Comic
Mrs. Gunnysack, could be any age

> *Mrs. Gunnysack is a high school drama teacher. Here, she is laying
> out the requirements to a classroom of high school students on the
> first day of Drama One.*

MRS. GUNNYSACK: Good morning everyone, good morning. Welcome to
Drama One. I'll be your teacher this quarter, Mrs. Gunnysack. But
call me Helen. Mrs. Gunnysack is my mother's name. Ha ha ha ha
ha. Enough horsing around. It's time to get down to business. What
business am I talking about? The business of *theater*.

Now, as you know, due to budget cuts across the state, all schools
have been forced to cut down on the number of sessions for all
nonessential subjects, including, but not limited to, History, English,
lunch and Drama. This year's restrictions will be even tighter than in
previous years, resulting in quite a low number of class sessions for
Drama — and by "low number" I of course mean "one."

And because class times have also been cut, it will only last twenty
minutes.

(She hears general hubbub from the class.)

Now now! That's enough hubbub. Before we proceed with class,
I have some additional news. Principal Trollybottom has informed
me that there will be a school-wide assembly at noon. And because
[Current month] is National Shakespeare Awareness Month, this
Drama class has been assigned to present a Shakespeare play for the
entire student body.

And our time slot at the assembly is only ten minutes.

(She recognizes that general hubbub is nearly beginning again.)

Now before you get all "frizzled," as I've heard the rap singers
say, let me tell you this: I've learned many crucial things throughout

my years in the theater. The crucialest among them is to always make the most out of what you're given. So while we only have twenty — *(She looks at her watch.)* — sorry, eighteen minutes to rehearse a full-length play that you'll end up performing during a ten-minute period — well — that's no obstacle for a *true* Thespian. No . . . Pressure is where the dramatic *thrive*. And by golly, *(Passionately whispered:)* by *golly* — we're going to put on the best darn play this school has ever seen! Now who's with me?!

(Silence.)

Oh. Well. Everyone's with me because it's . . . required. OK! Now let's get started quickly, because the time . . . is out of joint. For those unfamiliar with Shakespeare's work, I just made an amusing Shakespeare reference. That may happen from time to time. What can I say — it's in my blood. *(Beat.)* Out, damned spot! Out, I say! Ha ha ha ha ha!

(Nobody finds this funny.)

SARAH, SARAH
Daniel Goldfarb

Dramatic
Rochelle, eighteen

> *Rochelle is speaking to her future mother-in-law, who doesn't think
> Rochelle is good enough for her son, Arthur.*

ROCHELLE: For Godsakes, the buns cost ten cents each, Mrs. Grosberg. I
am sorry. I am sorry I am not as rich as you want me to be. I am
sorry that my father didn't leave us with more. We've thought of sell-
ing the house, many times. We think about it all the time. Don't think
we haven't. But it's complicated. All our memories of my dad are tied
up in it. And it's hard to just walk away from that. Even if it seems
sensible! . . .

Look, I want you to like me, Mrs. Grosberg. I do. Because I'm
not going anywhere, and life'll be a lot easier if we can be friends. I
love Arthur. I love him. I love your son. And he loves me. I know
I'm not perfect. I know my family seems pretty lousy on paper, and
I don't have the know-how to prove otherwise. I know rich is better
than poor. But I'm just eighteen, Mrs. Grosberg . . .

. . . I can do a lot of things, Mrs. Grosberg. But I can't make
myself rich. I can't make my daddy alive. And I can't make him more
responsible with his money when he was alive. I can tell you he was
great. And I loved him a lot. And I miss him a lot. I can tell you,
that, even though he maybe spent too much, he did it out of love.
And that he had enormous respect for the right things; for education, for culture. He came over from the Old Country when he was
nine, by himself Mrs. Grosberg, and worked. He worked hard. And
I promise you, I work hard too. I don't need big rings and cashmere
sweaters. If Arthur likes to buy them, if he's proud, as you say, fine.

But my needs and desires aren't that fancy. I believe in Arthur. I'm going to put school on hold and work to support him while he's finishing his philosophy degree. And I know, there aren't a lot of rich philosophers, Mrs. Grosberg, and that's OK by me —

THE SCENE
Theresa Rebeck

Seriocomic
Clea, early twenties

> *Clea is a beautiful, sexy, rather callow young woman. She has recently come to New York, and is "making the scene," going to parties and trying to make her way in this dark world. Here, she is talking to Lewis and Charlie, two friends whom she has just met at a party.*

CLEA: No no, I don't drink. My mother was an alcoholic. I mean, she was a wonderful woman and she really loved me but it's like alcohol is so deadly, I mean at these parties sometimes when I'm at a party like this? To stand around and watch everyone turn into zombies around me? It just really triggers me, you know? You go ahead. I mean, that's just for me, I don't impose that on people or anything. . . .

Because you know, I was at this party last week it was such a scene, there were so many people there. You know it was this young director, he's got like seven things going at once, Off Broadway, his father is somebody famous or something, and he's very hot, I'm serious, I think I read in *Variety* that he has seven different plays up. Can you imagine, the energy level of someone like that? Anyway, it was his birthday party, and they rented out the top two floors of this loft in Chelsea, it was this wild party, like surreal, and then at one point in the evening? I just realized, that everyone was just totally shit-faced. The whole party! Everybody was like slurring their words and this one guy was just leaning against the wall like he couldn't even stand up, it was just really disgusting and I got so triggered. I mean I don't want to be reactive in situations like that, I don't like to judge people on a really superficial level or anything but it was kind of horrifying. I mean, not that I — you know, drink, you should drink! Enjoy yourselves!

THE SCENE
Theresa Rebeck

Comic
Clea, early twenties

> *Clea is a beautiful, sexy, rather callow young woman. She has recently come to New York and is "making the scene," going to parties and trying to make her way in this dark world. Here, she is talking to two buddies whom she has just met at a party, named Lewis and Charlie. What she doesn't know is that the "Nazi priestess" with whom she has just interviewed for a job is Charlie's wife, Stella.*

CLEA: [I'm from] Ohio. Isn't that hilarious? Plus I just got here, like, what, six months ago? It's a lot, I mean, to get used to. But it's so alive, just walking down the street, the energy. I'm like from, you know, the middle of nowhere, and I land here and it's so much more intense than even you think. Not like I'm some sort of cornball. But more like I'm alert, you know, really on fire with how amazing it is to be here. Because my experience, already, and don't take this personally, but people here are like not awake. To what — I don't want to sound judgmental because that is so not what I'm about but like what I mean is, I had this job interview yesterday, or the day be — no yesterday, I'm pretty sure, I had this amazing opportunity to work on this talk show, not that I think television is really a good place for anyone but I'm like trying to be open, really open, and anyway the agency sends me in to talk to this person who is like, she does something, I can't even tell what it is, for this talk show, like these people go on the television and interview movie stars or you know important people. I mean when they describe it to me, I'm like that's cool, this could be an interesting job for a couple weeks or something, and this person, this woman who I'm supposed to be working for is like — she's the person who calls and makes sure that everyone is going to show up, she books, you know, she books people. . . .

So I'm walking around this television studio, and there's like lights and you know "people" and everyone is so phony and intense, you just want to puke, like, what is supposed to be going on in a place like that? It's just like a void, with a lot of color in it. Totally bizarre. And this woman is so into it. I mean everything is just do this, be perfect, and her name is like "Stella" of course, so everyone is screaming, "Stella — Stella — Stella" which was like hilarious — . . .

Right? Right? And she could not be more like a Nazi priestess or something, she is so worked up over these phone lists and high-lighting in blue and mint green who needs to get returned, who hasn't returned, just utter crap — oh and on top of it all, she's in the middle of one of those adoptions, she's one of those infertile women who is like adopting an abandoned baby from China and that is like a total intense trip for her, those calls go on the special list, like lists are the holy grail to this total Nazi, like the lists and the movie stars and this invisible baby in the middle of China is like, you know, life to her. It was a total — just kind of horrible, you know? And I'm like — look around you! This city is so alive and you're just like — I don't know. Wow I think that vodka just hit, I so don't drink. Do you know what I mean? About being alive, I mean?

THE SCENE
Theresa Rebeck

Comic
Stella, thirties to forties

*Stella books guests on a TV talk show. She has come home after a
particularly trying day and vents to her husband, Charlie, an out-
of-work actor.*

STELLA: I had a horrible day. . . .

That idiot not showing. Not your idiot. My idiot. Didn't show.
All the shit I had to go through to get her to do us, six dozen white
lilies in her dressing room, do you know what that many lilies smells
like? It's enough to truly knock you out, like a disease, that many
flowers. And I'm not even talking about all the stupid candy we had
to buy. M&Ms. Reese's Cups. Twix. Why do these people think it's
so cool to eat bad chocolate? Could someone, and I mean, I liter-
ally had to turn her fucking dressing room into a kind of physical
representation of a complete psychotic break, lilies and bad chocolate and an EXERCISE MACHINE — she was only supposed to
be in there for an hour and a half, and she needed her own STAIR-
MASTER, with the chocolate, what's the plan, to eat the mounds
of chocolate, while you're ON the stairmaster? Turns out there was
no plan, because — she didn't show. . . .

I told you eight times. I'm turning into one of those people who
say things over and over and then you have to tell them so kindly,
yes you told me, like they've gone senile — this happened to my
mother, after she turned fifty, she told the same story over and over
and over again, it was so dreary — it was like oh, and now Mom's
gone insane, she's not just a pathetic nut, now she's a boring pathetic
nut, telling the same story, over and over and over again — . . .

I'm half smashed already. That idiot didn't show. She did not
show! . . .

It is the fourth time, it is the fourth time she's fucked us and they insist that I book her anyway! And then it's my fucking fault we have a hole in the schedule. And there's not even a hole, I back us up every time with that idiot who makes the low-carb pasta dishes, why do people believe that? Low-carb pasta? Why do they — . . .

It's so, demeaning, to put that on television, it's just demeaning. These people are all such liars. Low-carb pasta? And it's pathetic, these women sitting out there, so hungry for this specific lie, you can eat pasta and still lose weight, that's like pathetic, it's not pathetic, it's sad, if you think about it too long, it is so sad all those women sitting out there in the house, their yearning for life to be just that little bit easier. It's probably one of the few things they have to look forward to, a nice plate of pasta with a little red sauce — only most of them, they don't go for the sensible red sauce, they go for the alfredo, or the carbonnara, I actually had to do a low-fat carbonnara show once. . . .

Oh God. I want to have compassion for these people, I feel bad — . . .

That they think this is a cool thing to do with their time, go and be the studio audience for a stupid talk show! . . .

Because they think it means something, to be on television — Only you weren't, really, you just sat there while someone else got to be on television. It's so sad. It's so so sad.

SCRAMBLED EGGS
Robin Amos Kahn and Gary Richards

Seriocomic
Karen, twenties to thirties

Karen confesses her fears about her marriage. Direct address to the audience.

KAREN: The limbo contest? I find one of those string hammocks and lie down. It actually feels like a straight jacket. I'm taking slow deep breaths, staring up at the bright, cloudless blue sky, wondering . . . what the hell is happening to me? *(Beat. As the sound of music fades, the lights change.)* When we get back to New York, it gets even worse. I keep forgetting things. Names. Appointments. I'm constantly using the wrong words for things like: "It's raining outside. Don't forget the elevator." I'm afraid to speak up in meetings. The phone rings and it's my friend Ruthie and I think, "Who the hell is Ruthie?" And I have no sex drive — zero — and I keep having these thoughts all night long. I spin scenarios, all disastrous — from global warming to terrorism to the amount of Sweet 'N Low I've consumed in my lifetime. I'm so depressed, antidepressants won't work on me. I'll have a nervous breakdown and then I'll have to go into a mental hospital. And everyone will look at Dave and say, "Poor Dave, his wife is nuts." And while I'm in the mental hospital, I'll get some kind of cancer, and after many horrible months of chemo, and radiation, and whatever experimental drugs they try, I'll die, and then Dave will be so depressed about my death, and about the Mets, that he'll kill himself, or . . . he won't kill himself, he'll find some hot young babe and on and on it goes and I can't stop it. I can't turn it off! ENOUGH!!!

SEZ SHE

Jane Martin

Comic
Actress, middle school age

*An eighth grader is upset by the way her mother has dressed to go
to the P.T.A. meeting.*

ACTRESS: Oh my God, Mom! You are not, I am completely serious, going
out of this house wearing that! Bitch me out. Do you know what you
look like? You are mega-embarrassing, OK? Mom! You are representing
me at the P.T.A., I can't have everybody's eighth grade parents seeing
you in hooker wear. Ohmygod. Do you know how old you are? You
are an ancient, decrepit person, Mom. Sorreee, but you are. Spaghetti
straps, and don't tell me that skirt passes the finger test, Mom! Wait
a minute, wait one minute, open your mouth and hold it open.
Ohmygod, gross! Ohmygod, is that a tongue piercing? Mother,
menopause and tongue piercing are polar opposites, OK? Mom, there
is a dress code, you can't walk into the P.T.A. direct from the whore
wars. God, Mom, have a little respect, will you, you're a dentist. I
mean where are we headed here I would like to ask. Are you going
to be one of those sixty-year-olds who look like steel prunes showing endless leg with plucked eyebrows and breast augmentation? I
warn you, Mom, if you set foot in the P.T.A. I will get Dad and Aunt
Lucy and your therapist and Father O'Keefe, and we'll do an inter-
vention in the parking lot. I mean hand over the tanning salon dis-
count coupons. You know, I'm sorry but the difference between who
you are and who you think you are is an unbelievable sag factor. Now
go upstairs this minute and put on something with long sleeves and
flats. You can go to the meeting but, after that, ohmygod, you are
soooo grounded!

SEZ SHE
Jane Martin

Comic
Actress, twenties to thirties

A young mother of three small children explains the usefulness of theater. When she goes, it's the only time she gets any sleep.

ACTRESS: I don't know about you but I go to the theater to get a little sleep. I know, you think I'm kidding. Listen here, I have three kids so you know there's no sleep to be had at home . . . babies crying, cats throwing up hairballs, dogs barking at moths and a husband who can only identify a sexual urge at the break of dawn. I have to seek out public events to get a little peace and quiet. Even that's become difficult. Until the late 50s you could sleep at the movies . . . that was pre-car chase. Squeal, roar, crash, fireball! Impossible. Symphony halls? They always throw in one piece of contemporary music scored for an outboard motor and two chain saws. Libraries? They think you're homeless. Museums? There's always a docent whispering in your ear. We are a universally sleep-deprived nation. We're irritable, socially aggressive, politically schizoid; we have got to get some sleep! I know you know what I'm talking about. Great sex is OK, but eight hours of uninterrupted sleep is unbelievably erotic. I'm sorry, I'm sorry, I'm a little edgy. Are my hands shaking? My eyes are red, right? I am telling you, the theater is the only place left to sleep. The soporific sound of endless conversation, kind of white noise, a sort of verbal sea sound. Lulling situations you've seen a thousand times . . . delicious boredom. They talk for a long time and then they get divorced or they die a lingering death or they decide to . . . I don't know . . . live lives of quiet desperation. If it's Chekhov, there are fabulous pauses, one right after the other. Or Iambic pentameter, God, that would put anybody to sleep. But here's the best part, nobody ever wakes you because a) it's socially embarrassing or b) they're asleep, too. One time, a thoughtful woman next to me put her coat over me during King Lear and sang this really quiet lullaby — it was so touching. Sure, it's a little expensive, but hey, you wake up to applause . . . if you're disoriented the ushers are really nice about helping you out of the theater. Once they just turned out the lights and left me there until morning. You could try it now. Go ahead. The next piece is really quiet and sort of hypnotic. Don't be shy, really. I'll get the actors to hold it down. Shhhh. Rockabye.

SEZ SHE
Jane Martin

Comic
Actress, could be any age

An actress talks to her audience about ways they can a better audience.

ACTRESS: Not bad at all. Really good. Keepers, we would call you keepers . . . the other actresses and myself . . . concerning you . . . in your capacity as an audience. We find you . . . giving, spontaneous . . . very intelligent, very intelligent, willing to laugh, very important, amazingly important. We . . . we actresses, together, well we have worked with, what . . . many, many audiences. I don't know if you know we judge and compare you. We do. The critics analyze us; we analyze you. Afterwards we, you know, have a beer or a, uh . . . cranberry juice, and we go over you with a fine-tooth comb . . . no, really, we do, we pick you apart concerning your skills and deportment. Affectionately. I'm not saying it isn't affectionate. And you'll do well. This audience gets good reviews . . . except . . . I don't even know if I should bring this up. Should I bring this up? . . . OK. You're not breathing. You're forgetting to breathe. Breathing is your responsibility as an audience. See, when you're breathing, you're in a receptive state, your senses and intellect take in, but when you don't breathe, you are rejecting . . . experience . . . denying it. See, that would be bad for us, bad for the narrative. We would hate that. Right? . . . When you breathe, you are aware of the world that is not yourself. It's the reminder that you exist in-relation-to. You recognize yourself, you recognize the other, which closes the circle and creates . . . well . . . coherence. It's a big job. If you remembered to breathe, you would do it 14,880 times a day. Not breathing would, practically speaking, mean you were dead, which kind of means doing a play for you would be . . . well beside the point. *(Sudden awareness.)* Shoot! Can you believe it? I forgot to breathe. I forgot to breathe even though I was talking about breath. Bummer. I was worried that you would think this doesn't belong in a play and, while I did that, you disappeared and I disappeared and all that was present was worry. Terrible. That's terrible of me. I mean to communicate the play I would have to be present. Whoa! Let's go back on track here. Breathe in. Breathe out. Breathe in, breathe out. Breathe in, breathe out. Ah. See, now the play's between us. Breathe again. Oh, that's much better.

SEZ SHE
Jane Martin

Seriocomic
Actress, a college student

A young college student confronts her history professor.

ACTRESS: Professor Drysdale? Professor Drysdale? I'm terribly sorry to come puffing up to you all out of breath like this, but I had a question about Rome, really. I'm not keeping you from class, am I? Oh good, I would hate to be a nuisance. I'm not imposing, am I? Oh, double good. You see I seem to have lost or incorrectly discarded or mistakenly eaten my January 17th notes, and I'm completely flummoxed as to whether it was Scipio or Cato who died in exile? Oh good, Scipio, right, well that clears that right up, I was so flummoxed. Wait, Professor Drysdale, one more question, just one, I promise. I wondered if we'd be taking off our clothes again anytime soon? I'm not speaking too loudly, am I? Because if we were, if that was on the schedule, I think I'd like to be conscious this time. Just for the experience. Because that drink you gave me, well, I just wasn't really aware of all the fun we must have had after that, and now that I've been *(How did Curio the Younger put it?)* deflowered, I was hoping to be present the next time, and get the full effect. Hi, Sally, hi, Alexander! Oh really? No, I don't think I can make it to the study group because as far as I know, Professor Drysdale will be sexually harassing me this evening. I know, he looks kind of old and wizened, but that doesn't matter because, luckily he has knockout drops which skims us right past the age difference. Bye. So I could probably meet you around six because I have a meeting with Dean Montgomery at four, nothing academic, just a little personal problem, but it won't take too long. So, anyway, we could discuss the aqueducts and Hadrian, and then you could take advantage of me, which might get a little kinky because I'll be wired this time. Bye, Professor Drysdale. Can't wait. See you. Bye. Quo Vadis.

SHAKESPEARE IN HOLLYWOOD
Ken Ludwig

Comic
Olivia, twenties

> *Olivia is a 30s Hollywood movie starlet, cast as Hermia in what is to become Max Reinhardt's legendary film of* A Midsummer Night's Dream. *She is unprepared for today's filming and explains to a guy she thinks is another actor that she needs to lay low for a while to try and learn her lines. The guy she's talking to is Oberon. The* real *Oberon, from the play, who has wandered on to the set.*

OLIVIA: I'm in this movie. I play Hermia. And I fought so hard to get the role, you have no idea! I did screen test after screen test, and I memorized the entire part. Only a different part. I wanted to play Puck. . . .

I know, you think a boy should play him, but until this century, Puck was always a girl. . . .

Anyway, I got the part of Hermia, which is tremendous, it's the biggest break I ever had, and of course to play opposite Dick Powell, the biggest heartthrob in Hollywood, he's such a sweetheart, God in heaven, but I was going to really memorize the lines last night, at least get a start and learn the ones for today, but then my brother got a cable from his base that he was being sent to flight school in the morning! So anyway, we stayed up the entire night so we could spend a few more hours together, and we tried to make a party of it, and I guess I got a little drunk and then I woke up this morning and I hadn't learned the lines, at least the way I want to, and I just can't bear to face the great Max Reinhardt without being well prepared, so I'm hiding out to get some time alone so I can memorize it better since I'd look like such a fool if I didn't know it really well, do you see?

SHOW PEOPLE
Paul Weitz

Comic
Natalie, twenties

> *Natalie is an aspiring actress who's been hired by a wealthy, eccen-*
> *tric young man to impersonate his fiancée during a weekend at his*
> *posh Hamptons beach house. He needs a "fiancée" to meet his par-*
> *ents, who are also visiting. Natalie has found out that the "parents"*
> *are also actors, hired to play the parents for the weekend. They were*
> *once regularly on Broadway, but they haven't had jobs for years. Be-*
> *cause they are experienced actors, though, Natalie asks the "Mom,"*
> *Marnie, for advice, and for reassurance.*

NATALIE: Do you think I'm a good actress? . . .

I came to New York six years ago to be an actress, and . . . this year, my only role was I played a topless horse in an avant-garde play based on Picasso's *Guernica*. . . .

I mean, I was topless, in the role. The director talked me into it. He wanted me completely nude, but I drew the line. . . .

So I'm prancing around on stage with my boobs hanging out, snorting and kicking, when I see my stepfather in the audience. He hasn't seen me act since the first grade. He never came to any of the high school musicals. But he was in New York for the weekend for a Toyota sales convention. And he decided to surprise me by coming to my play, because I sent my mother a postcard about it. Now he's sitting in an audience of ten people, who are outnumbered by the actors, and I've got my tits exposed, I'm neighing, making a complete idiot of myself. And the worst thing was, after the performance, he told me he never knew I had that much talent. . . .

So anyway, after the stepfather thing I decided that was it, I was going to quit acting and go back to Columbus, and start a muffin business called "Magnificent Muffins." I've always liked baking, and . . . look at Mrs. Fields. But the only thing is . . . I've tasted Mrs. Fields, I like Mrs. Fields and . . . I'm no Mrs. Fields. . . .

You're an actress. I mean a real actress. You've been on Broadway. In straight plays.

You're like some magnificent dinosaur. . . .

The stage is your home. . . .

You see you've . . . you've lived my dream.

I mean I guess you're . . . not doing so well financially, or you wouldn't be here. And maybe you have a problem with alcohol, and maybe you're bitter about how your career and your life have gone, but so what? At least you've lived on the stage. I'd go through all that and more just to be a real actress.

SHOW PEOPLE
Paul Weitz

Dramatic, with a tinge of seriocomic
Marnie, fifties to sixties

> *Once a fairly successful Broadway actress, Marnie hasn't worked in*
> *years. She and her husband, also an actor, have been hired by an*
> *eccentric, wealthy young man to impersonate his parents during a*
> *weekend at his Hamptons beach house. Reluctant at first to give this*
> *her all, Marnie is finally provoked into telling off her "son."*

MARNIE: Now listen here, you little bastard. You think you had a hard time
having *us* as parents? Well try having *you* for a son! . . .

    You were a sullen little creature, from the day you were born.
No *before* that. Do you know the *hours* we spent reading to you while
you were in the womb? We read you poetry. Yeats. Rilke — in the
original German! We read you *Robert Frost,* dammit! And I *hate* Robert
Frost. I went through a *twenty-three* hour labor with you, you were
so reluctant to face the world, it was like giving birth to a *mule!* And
when you finally *did* emerge, I've never seen a less lovable baby! You
never smiled, never laughed. You used to cry, wail at the top of your
lungs, until one of us came rushing in at four in the morning, then
you'd stop crying immediately, and you'd stare at us, with this un-
pleasant, critical expression on your face. You know what your first
word was? . . .

    No. We just *told* you it was Dada. But really, it was "Mine!" You
used to sit there in your crib, saying "Mine! Mine! Mine! Mine!" You
were an *ugly* baby. And a bully. We couldn't put you in a crib with
another child, because you'd pinch them. But *still* we loved you. . . .

    Your father was so proud. His face beamed when he was around
you. You could *feel* his heart swelling up with love for his son. It was
something he wanted his whole life. A *child.* We tried, and tried, had

our hopes raised up and dashed, so many times, and finally, just when we'd give up hope, *you* arrived. . . .

You arrived, and you broke our hearts. Well, you know what, I'm *glad* we never had children. I'm glad, Jerry. Because *this* is how they end up!

SIN
(A CARDINAL DEPOSED)
Michael Murphy

Dramatic
Maryetta Dussourd, thirties to forties

> Sin *is about the trial of an American Roman Catholic Cardinal*
> *accused of covering up allegations of sexual abuse by priests in his*
> *archdiocese. This is the deposition of the mother of one of the mo-*
> *lested boys.*

MARYETTA: Um, Father Geoghan invited himself to our home so he could get to know the family. Which — any priest that's child orientated . . . He was CYO, he had the altar boys he was in charge of. That seems perfectly natural. He's around children all the time. So he came and he dropped down to meet the family. And it just became he'd drop in when he wanted to drop in. He'd talk to me about the prayer group, um, and things like that, how he could be a help with the children. So he seemed like he was a friend. Um. The way that I found out was that my sister made a phone call to me and she had told me that my sons had been raped by Father John Geoghan. And that I needed to speak to my sons. And that's how I found out. And immediately after, I took the older child and I separated him and I talked with him. And . . . My child became filled with fear. He was crying and shaking. He told me that Father John Geoghan said that I wouldn't believe him. That I . . . had too much faith in the church . . . and that I wouldn't believe him. And then my son told me how things happened. He told me how Father Geoghan threatened him. And immediately my child tried to run out our back door — and I, I pulled my son back and I told my son that I would never, ever stop loving him. And I told my son that no way could Father Geoghan ever separate us. Well, the thing is, it separated us, it separated everybody in that . . . I felt so guilty. I would dress my little four-year-old and my little six-year-old and nine-year-old and feed them, and thinking I was loving them so much and they would just look at you with the littlest, sweetest faces. And I caused their violation. If I hadn't invited that man into my house . . . I'm the reason all of this has happened to everybody. I'm the guilty person. Um . . . And I had to take care of it. And I did that. And I knew the vicar of this area and I went to that person. And he was overwhelmed. Because it was the first time he had ever heard of it. And he invited Father John Geoghan down to his house, to the rectory, had lunch with him. They sat across the table from each other, and when he asked Father John Geoghan — Father John Geoghan readily admitted it. And he said to the vicar, oh, well, it was only two families.

ST. SCARLET
Julia Jordan

Dramatic
Rose, twenty-nine

> *Rose's mother has recently died. Here, she is talking to Vinnie, a strange man from New York with whom she once had a one-night stand.*

ROSE: We didn't get along so well. She was real buttoned up. Me, I'm more like my dad. She was always trying to shut me down. Kicked me out when I was seventeen. . . .

   There was this boy and . . . I don't know. He had perfect skin. My hands shook when I touched it, it, like, glowed so hard. And he dared me . . . We got caught together on the convent lawn. It was a pretty effective fuck you, considering the fact she taught at the school. So then there was a fight and I told her I didn't have to take that shit, and she said, "Leave then," and I did. Left for bigger places and other boys, in bars and clubs with spinning lights. Lights that spun so hard. And those lights were beautiful to me, can't explain it, but they were, for a while. 'Til my eyes adjusted. But then it was just someone else, someplace else. And on and on like that 'til skin was just skin again. No light inside it. No glow at all. Convent lawn boy? Taken over his dad's hardware store. God, he looks dull. Didn't remember my name. Not off the top of his head. At least he recognized me. My mom didn't, or only half did. Sometimes. You've come all this way and made up this big thing and . . . Look, I slept with you and I barely remember you. Why would you want someone like that?

TATJANA IN COLOR
Julia Jordan

Dramatic
Tatjana, twelve

> *Tatjana is talking to the Painter Egon Schiele about her namesake,*
> *the Patron Saint of students.*

TATJANA: When Saint Martyress Tatjana died, it was extraordinary. . . .

She was very rich. And had everything, furs and silks and banquets and feasts. But she didn't care a fig for any of it. She wanted to be a saint. . . .

She just could not help it. She was so saintly she gave away everything she had to the poor and deprived. And they had never tasted anything as sweet as the cakes she lavished on them. And they had never felt anything so soft as her dresses of velvet and silk. She made them happy. . . .

She wore the rags of the poor and deprived, which scratched her skin. . . .

And she tended to the sick and visited people in dungeons to cheer them up and pray for them. . . .

And she liked to pray. She apparently did a lot of praying. But on top of all that, she was beautiful, the most beautiful girl anyone had ever seen. . . .

The emperor wanted to marry her. But he worshipped Apollo . . .

She would not marry him. She would not wear a crown and a purple velvet robe and worship the sun. It would have gotten in the way of the proper praying. . . .

She refused him. So the emperor tortured her with iron hooks, but still she would not renounce God. The emperor threw her into his dungeon, that she had so often visited before to comfort others. But she was alone. And it was dark. And damp. And cold. But suddenly, the walls started to glow and there was a beautiful warm light on her face. A shimmering that she could not only see, but feel and hear and almost taste. It was an angel. And the shimmering she felt, were her wounds being healed. The next day she walked out of the dungeon, more beautiful than ever. For you see, there was a tiny bit of angel glow still left on her skin. And the emperor wanted to marry her more than ever. But when he asked for her hand, she declined for the second time because she loved God and was promptly boiled in oil. He wanted to burn the light off her skin. But she didn't die, just got scalded a bit. And the angel came to her dungeon and healed her wounds a second time. So you can imagine what happened . . .

. . . he dragged her through the streets behind a team of ice-white horses! But she lived to see the angel of the dungeon a third time. But this time she was extremely tired, as you can imagine. So she prayed to the angel and to God to not save her a third time. But let her die and join them in heaven. But the angel did not answer and she steeled herself for more torture when she walked out of the dungeon, so beautiful, so full of light that even the emperor, who worshipped the sun, could barely look at her. He asked for her hand and she said . . . "No, I am married to God. I will never betray him." So he cut off her head. And she got her wish. The angel let her die and join them in heaven. And that is how Tatjana became the martyress and patron saint of students. The end.

THE THEODORE ROOSEVELT ROTUNDA

Jennifer Camp

Seriocomic
Lillian, British, forties

> *Lillian is a literature professor. Here, she talks to the audience about how the Museum of Natural History in New York symbolizes America and Americans.*

LILLIAN: I cannot understand why the Americans have such a fascination with the bottom. Kick your ass. We really kicked butt. Whup yur ass. Kiss my ass. I've been here for almost six months and no one's been able to explain it to me. It's baffling. I mean, it's all either got to do with kicking or kissing. Sex and violence. That's what drew me to this place. It's full of sex and violence. In Virginia Woolf's novel *Mrs. Dalloway,* of which I'm somewhat of an expert, there's a passage which reads, " . . . she always had the feeling that it was very, very dangerous to live even one day." I quite agree. Mildred was against my coming to New York from the beginning. Mildred says I'm an avoider. *Avoider.* I don't even think that's a word. She said to me the day before I left, she said, "You're like Oedipus, Lillian. You're running and running and running and one day you're going to discover that what you're running from is you. That *you* are the person you seek." I hate Mildred. but she's right. I do have one form of movement and it's forward. That doesn't really explain, of course, why I find I can't actually go *in* the museum. That I stop in the lobby. Perhaps I'm just not quite up to facing it all. I mean, is one meant to assume that The Museum of Natural History implies the natural history of *everything*? That's a rather lofty aim, isn't it? Some mornings I can't even bear to look in the mirror so I hardly think I should be prepared to face the entire natural history of everything.

THOSE WHO CAN, DO
Brighde Mullins

Dramatic
Ann Marie, mid-thirties

*The Staten Island Ferry. Ann Marie comes to terms with leaving
her job as a teacher and returning to advertising.*

ANN MARIE: In Italy they call their teachers "maestro." In Ireland the teacher
is the town hero. In Jewish culture the teacher is heaped with praise.
In America you're the Village Idiot, the "One Who Can't," over-
worked, invisible until targeted, surrounded by the inept and saddled
with the Walking Wounded, the casualties of an uncivilized civiliza-
tion. Yes, I fled. Yes. It was all a learning experience. One thing that
I learned is that there is some validity in the well-worn phrase, the
saying handed down. The phrase that cropped up for me, even as I
was flailing was "no one is my enemy, no one is my friend, everyone
is my teacher." It's a nice thought, anyway. Neutralizes the paranoia.
Maybe that's what my shrink meant when she said that Celia freaked
me out because of . . . I don't know. I am all right with Not Knowing. I don't need to know why she bothered me so much. Was she
dangerous? Did I take her manias too personally? It's my life. I have
to take it personally.
   (Tiny beat.)
   I still take the Ferry some nights, just to see the proximity of the
moon, hear the screams of gulls, see the silhouette of the skyline. My
idealism ended in a court-case, my career change ended in stretch
marks, no matter! I learned some things.
   (Little pause.)
   I sit on the top deck of the Ferry. When it nudges into port in
Staten Island, I don't get off. I wait. I simply wait. It will reverse direction. After ten minutes the heft of the ferry churns back to Man-
hattan, where I still feel safe just walking around.
   (Sounds in: the city, its sirens, subway noises.)

WATERBORN
Edith L. Freni

Dramatic
Leslie, twenties

Leslie is explaining to her husband, Mark, about why "natural child-birth" is not for her.

LESLIE: *Magic* is pulling rabbits out of hats and making decks of cards appear out of thin air which . . . would be great in the case of babies but alas it is not magic that causes perfectly normal women to grunt and scream and BLEED PROFUSELY and totally lose bowel control before forcing something the size of a rabbit out of something the size of a deck of cards. THAT is just "the way it is" and THAT does not sound like so much fun to me, in fact, it's always sounded like a rather humiliating way to spend six to twenty-four hours. So, you'll forgive me, but if I'm gonna have to go through all that shit, I don't want to be conscious of its happening. I don't want to *feel* it or *experience* it — I'll tell you what I want — I want a hospital gown, a bed and strong painkillers. I want a *doctor*, a couple nurses maybe — all female by the way — and I want you in the waiting room, pacing back and forth with a cigar in your shirt pocket just like my father did. No camcorders pointed at my fucking cunt, no sweat-drenched hair stroking, I-love-you-so-much-honeys. No weepy moments after it's all over and certainly no visitors while I recoup. Sorry but this chick, not into it. Blame my mother if you wanna blame someone but don't look at me 'cause you knew I was this way when we got married.

WHAT ANDY WARHOL
NEVER TOLD ME
Robert Pridham

Seriocomic
Shawanda, ten to fourteen

> *For one group of middle school girls, becoming famous is an*
> *all-consuming goal. Here, Shawanda describes her unexpected brush*
> *with fame.*

SHAWANDA: My Fifteen Minutes of Fame, by Shawanda Cleese.

Andy Warhol was a famous American artist who painted pictures of soup cans and Marilyn Monroe and Jackie Kennedy and other famous people, and you can still see his paintings in museums all over the world. But he was also famous for some of the things he said, and one of the most famous things he said was that, sooner or later, everyone in the world would be famous for fifteen minutes. And he was right, because my fifteen minutes happened to me last summer. But what Andy Warhol forgot to say was that you never know when your fifteen minutes are going to happen, and if you aren't ready and don't know how to make the best of them, your fifteen minutes will be over and only your normal old life will be left. So don't miss your chance! Be prepared!!! Because I, Shawanda Cleese, am living proof that your fifteen minutes can sneak up on you when you least expect them.

One Sunday morning, I went to the corner store on our street to get the Sunday newspaper for my father and one of those big, boxy things of orange juice for my mom and little sister. I like to go to the store on Sunday morning — it's my time for myself. But on this particular Sunday morning, I could see a whole lot of people on the corner and a couple of big trucks and lights and electric wires running all over the street and I could hear somebody yelling — sounded like into a microphone or something. I went up to the corner to see what was going on and when I looked down where the lights were pointing, I could see a bunch of people at the end of the street, and a man sitting in a seat on the top of a crane, talking to them.

And then I saw the cameras.

Next thing I know, the crane man shouts "Action!" and all those people at the end of the street start screaming their lungs out and running right toward where I'm standing. And then they stopped, and the director — see I'd figured out by then that the crane man was the director — starts yelling: "It's not right!! It's not right!! It's not what I want, people! It doesn't have the pa-thos" — that's what he said, pa-thos — "It doesn't have the pa-thos!" Boy, he was having just about one of the worst temper tantrums I've ever seen. And right at that very moment, he spots me standing in the crowd, and he points right at me and he shouts: "There she is! There's my pa-thos!"

Well, I don't know what he's talking about, but the next thing I know there's all these movie people around me asking me if I want to be in the movie too and if my parents will let me, and I tell them sure, my parents won't mind that I get to be in a movie and pretty soon I'm standing at the other end of the street with all the other people and what I'm supposed to do is this:

When everyone starts yelling and running, I'm supposed to stay behind with my box of orange juice and start crying "Where's my mommy? Where's my mommy?" real sad and scared-like, and then I kind of turn around and look up and get this really, really horrified expression on my face, just like I see something so awful I can't even find the words to describe it — like this:

(She makes the face for us.)

— and then I scream and fall down dead in a faint, like this:

(She screams and falls down dead in a faint, then pops back up.)

So I do all of that three times, and I'm getting to be really good at it — I mean, watch out Angelina Jolie! — and the director says: "That's fine, that's just the right pa-thos I need! Why, just as soon as we add in all of the computerized special effects, it'll be perfect!"

So, finally, almost a year later, we go to see the movie, right? My mother and father, all of my friends, even my Aunt Neddie — everybody goes to see me in my first movie. I mean, there are so many of us, we practically fill up the whole theater. And there I am, up on the big screen — and you can see me just over to the right, there, with all the other people, running and screaming — and here comes my big line: you can see me opening my mouth and I start to say "Where's my — "

And right then, right at that very moment, this gigantic, humongous Godzilla foot comes right down on top of me — I mean, this thing is huge — and it squishes me right into the road. Flat. Smooshed. Pancake-city. Right in the middle of my line.

And that's the story of my fifteen minutes. So when Andy Warhol says everybody is going to be famous for fifteen minutes, he's right. But he better tell everybody to be ready, because you never know when those fifteen minutes will come — and if you're not careful, your fifteen minutes will get smooshed in the road, just like mine.

WHAT ANDY WARHOL NEVER TOLD ME

Robert Pridham

Comic
Lisa, ten to fourteen

> *For one group of middle school girls, become famous is an all-consuming goal. Here, Lisa describes the ups and downs of overnight stardom.*

LISA: The thing about being famous is that you get to have everything the way you want it. You get to be in control. You get to tell people to do things the way you want them done. I don't like those flowers in the living room. Poof! The flowers are gone. I want shrimp for dinner, not chicken. Poof! You have shrimp. I don't like my room anymore, my house, my yard. Poof! Poof! Poof! It's interesting when you think about it, because the only reason you're famous is because other people make you famous. The thing I want to know is: How do you get other people to do that? How do you get them to decide you're famous and somebody else isn't? I mean, is it like earning points or something, and once you have enough of them somebody says, hey, she just earned enough points to move up from being pretty well known to being famous so let's take her picture and put her on the cover of a magazine. And what happens if you decide you don't want to be famous any more. Like, say you want to go out for some chicken fingers and a soda, and you can't because you're famous and other people will stare at you while you're eating. Or you want to shop at your favorite store at the mall but you can't because you're famous and other people will watch you changing your clothes. Do you just get to decide you're tired of being famous and you want to go back to being your same old ordinary self again? I mean, it's not like you can send an announcement to the papers and the magazines and say: Hey, sorry, but I, Lisa Linders, do NOT want to be famous anymore, so everybody'd better just leave me alone, OK! Because, if you did that, you would probably wind up making yourself even more famous than you were before, and things would just get worse. I mean, people would be saying: Look! there goes that famous girl who decided she didn't want to be famous anymore, let's go get her autograph!

You'd be trapped.

WILD TURKEYS
Don Nigro

Dramatic
Miranda, sixteen

> *This is the complete text of this short monologue play. Lights up on Miranda Tully, age sixteen, sitting in her own circle of light on an otherwise dark stage, wearing a T-shirt and panties, in the morning.*

MIRANDA: They stood in the yard by the woods again this morning.
Seven wild turkeys, shambling along
like spectral old ladies with buzzardy eyes.
They come in the fog and stalk up the hillside
and through the trees, plodding, phlegmatic,
keeping together, mumbling to one another
like mourners at a funeral. They're taller
than I thought they'd be, and more strange.
I don't know where they come from.
They come more often now on foggy mornings,
They seem very pre-occupied, as if
they're waiting for something.
I don't know what it is.
What are they thinking about?
I get up early in tee shirt and panties to vomit,
then have a glass of apple juice,
and find myself drawn compulsively to the window.
I pull back the the curtain and peer out,
and there they are, as I knew they'd be.
I stand by the window and stare at them.
My bare feet and legs are cold,
but I can't seem to turn away.
They're not looking in my direction,

but they know I'm here.
Am I the reason they've come?
The wild turkeys mill about in the fog
as if one of them's lost his pocket watch.
I want to go outside. I don't care that it's cold.
I want to go up the hill and talk to them.
But something makes me hesitate.
The first one I saw, some days ago,
was a smaller one, wandering alone out there.
It seemed to be lost. I was concerned.
I walked up the hill, right toward it.
I expected the thing to scurry up into the woods,
but the creature just looked at me.
No fear. No anger. Not curiosity, quite.
Perhaps just a hint of expectation.
It looked at me for the longest time,
and I looked back. And then, for the first time,
I felt something moving inside me.
Then the monster turned, as if dismissing me,
or deciding with mild regret that I
had nothing much to offer him that day,
and made its way deliberately through the bushes
and up the ravaged hillside. No rush.
One clawfoot step and then another. Such
ugly feet and beak, such a hideous red thing
hanging down like a stream of blood.
And yet a kind of awkward, eerie, ancient
hideous beauty there.
Lately, more and more, I have been feeling
this nearly overpowering compulsion
to go outside and find out what they want.
Do they want me to follow them?
Is that why they've come?
Is there something they want me to do, or see?
Or understand? Or have the creatures come
for what's inside me? If I followed them

up into the labyrinth of fallen woods,
where would they take me? What
would they do with me? Would they claw
between my legs? Last night I think I dreamed
of a clearing near the top of the wooded hillside
strewn with fallen trees and the bones of others
they've lured there. And in what I think
must be the lingering memory of this dream
I can see the wild turkeys standing over
a little corpse in the weeds.
The eye sockets of the little thing are empty,
the bones of the rib cage picked quite clean.
The turkeys stand around the wretched lost
child-thing's remains and look at me.
And I look in their eyes and suddenly
I know what they're trying to say to me.
Make a wish, they say.
On behalf of the darkly wattled gobbling
black carnivorous god
of all the wild turkeys of the noble
ancient dying east Ohio woods,
we, the ushers of this place,
invite you to make a wish.
You can't have her, I say, clutching
my stomach with both hands under my shirt.
You can't have her.
She's mine. She's mine.
*(Miranda sits there, touching her stomach tenderly under her T-shirt
with the palms of her hands. The light fades on her and goes out.)*

Inc., which has published the entire text in an acting edition and which handles performance rights. Contact info: 866-NEW-PLAY (phone); info@playscripts.com (E-mail); www.playscripts.com

NEVER TELL. ©2006 by James Christy. Reprinted by permission of Playscripts, Inc., which has published the entire text in an acting edition and which handles performance rights. Contact info: 866-NEW-PLAY (phone); info@playscripts.com (E-mail); www.playscripts.com

99 HISTORIES. ©2005 by Julia Cho. Reprinted by permission of John Buzzetti, The Gersh Agency, 41 Madison Ave., New York, NY 10010. The entire text has been published in an acting edition by Dramatists Play Service, 440 Park Ave. S., New York, NY 10016 (212-MU3-8960; www.dramatists.com) which also handles performance rights.

PARADISE. ©2003 by Glyn O'Malley. Reprinted by permission of the author. The entire text has been published in an acting edition by New York Theatre Experience in *Plays and Playwrights 2006.* Order online at www.nyte.org. For performance rights, contact Ronald Feiner, Kaufman, Feiner, Yamin, Gilden & Robbins LLC, 777 3rd Ave., New York, NY 10017.

POODLE WITH GUITAR AND DARK GLASSES. ©2005 by Liz Duffy Adams. Reprinted by permission of Playscripts, Inc., which has published the entire text in an acting edition and which handles performance rights. Contact info: 866-NEW-PLAY (phone); info@playscripts.com (E-mail); www.playscripts.com

QUEEN MILLI OF GALT. ©2005 by Gary Kirkham. Reprinted by permission of the author. The entire text has been published in an acting edition by Samuel French, Inc., 45 W. 25th St., New York, NY 10010 (212-206-8990; www.samuelfrench.com), which also handles performance rights.

ROMEO TO GO. ©2005 by Jonathan Rand. Reprinted by permission of Playscripts, Inc., which has published the entire text in an acting edition and which handles performance rights. Contact info: 866-NEW-PLAY (phone); info@playscripts.com (E-mail); www.playscripts.com

SARAH, SARAH. ©2005 by Daniel Goldfarb. Reprinted by permission of the author c/o Carl Mulert, The Gersh Agency, 41 Madison Ave., New York, NY 10010. The entire text has been published in an acting edition by Dramatists Play Service, 440 Park Ave. S., New York, NY 10016 (212-MU3-8960; www.dramatists.com) which also handles performance rights.

THE SCENE. © 2006 by Theresa Rebeck. Reprinted by permission of the